beaded crazy quilting

Cindy Gorder

©2005 Cindy Gorder
Published by

krause publications
An Imprint of F+W Publications

700 East State Street • Iola, WI 54990-0001
715-445-2214 • 888-457-2873

Our toll-free number to place an order or obtain a free catalog is 800-258-0929.

Nymo®, Silamide®, Kevlar®, Fine Braid™ by Kreinik, Thread Heaven®

Library of Congress Catalog Number: 2005930576

ISBN-13: 978-0-87349-892-0
ISBN-10: 0-87349-892-5

Edited by: Candy Wiza
Designed by Donna Mummery

Printed in China

Contents

Dedication

To Dick — my husband, best friend and love of my life.

Acknowledgments

I would like to thank the following:

My mother and grandmothers, who showed me the magic of using needle and thread.

Julie Stephani, without whose encouragement this book would not have been written.

Candy Wiza, my patient and understanding editor.

Introduction

I love the appeal of "no rules" for crazy patchwork, but I realize some people need some guidelines, at least to get started. So here in this book is what I've learned and observed during my crazy beaded patchwork journey. I hope it will help and inspire you to jump in and get started on your own adventure!

As you learn techniques for stitches and beadwork, keep in mind that everything can be modified, interchanged and combined in infinite ways. In fact, I encourage you to modify these projects in any way to suit your own sense of color and utilize the materials in your own collection.

Because no two stashes are alike, you'll need to substitute your own materials in the projects you create. With so many choices, you should have no trouble finding just the right fabric, thread or bead to make it uniquely yours!

I have been collecting beads, fabrics, threads, trims, ribbons and fibers for many years, and all of these projects were created from the materials in my stash. I believe you are twice rewarded when you become a collector: first when you find the prized material and later when you incorporate it into a work of art!

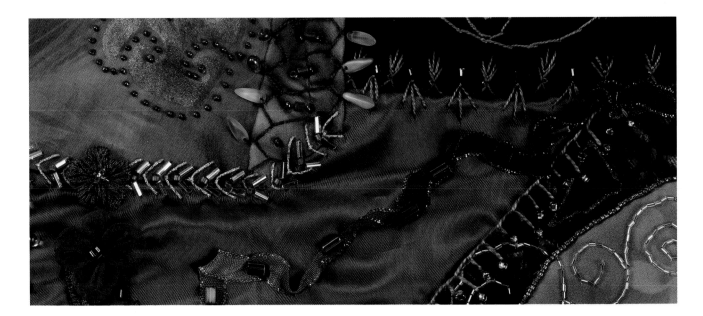

Supplies and Tools

Fabric for Motifs and Patches

Here's my rule — use whatever fabric you like. Use small scraps left over from sewing, crafting or other projects involving cloth. When shopping, buy small amounts of fabric. A quarter yard is usually 9" by 45", and from that you get a LOT of patches!

On average, when I'm creating a motif patch, I'll use a piece of fabric roughly 6" square, figuring an inch will be used for seam allowances and another inch or so will be the space between the motif and the border. The motif itself would be approximately 4" square, or 2" smaller than the patch. This isn't a hard and fast rule, just a general guideline.

When it comes to fiber content, buy what appeals to you. I love velvets and silks, but that's my personal preference. Sheer fabric, such as organza, may not be the best choice for beadwork (think of all the threads usually hidden at the back, showing through!) although it does look wonderful layered over solid fabric. So, if you fall in love with a sheer fabric, there are ways you can make it work.

Fabric ribbon is great for patches — you only use a 3" or 4" piece to fill in a small area. Imagine how far a yard of pretty ribbon might go in crazy patchwork. If the ribbon happens to come with wire edges, simply pull the wire out — or leave it in to sculpt a ribbon "wave" across the surface. Most ribbons have finished edges so they don't have to be turned under — what a timesaver!

I do have one guideline concerning fabric — use highly patterned fabrics sparingly. The stitching and embellishing are what you are showcasing and a wildly printed background is difficult to contrast with your embroidery and beadwork. You don't have to avoid them, just treat them as accents. Try to surround them with solid patches which will show off your fancy stitching.

Foundations

For individual motif patches, use fusible interfacing on the back to give the fabric extra support for the beadwork. The interfacing may be traced with a pattern prior to fusing it to the fabric, providing a stitching guide. Interfacing makes the fabric sturdy so you won't need an embroidery hoop.

The foundation of a crazy quilt can be fabric, such as muslin. My personal favorite is a thin, dense quilt batting. The batting has plenty of body and it retains its shape so an embroidery hoop isn't necessary.

Needles

Keep a variety of sizes on hand so you can use whatever works best for each situation. Needles will eventually wear out and break — usually at the eye — so keep extras on hand.

Use embroidery and/or chenille needles with a fairly large eye and sharp tip for embroidery and silk ribbon embroidery.

For beading, size 12 needles will work for most size 11/0 (the most common size) or larger seed beads. For size 15/0 seed beads and micro tubes, use a size 15 needle. (The smaller the bead/needle the larger the number size.) An assortment of sizes will come in handy. Beading needles can become bent with use. If they still perform satisfactorily, you can continue using them until they break. (All beading needles eventually break.) Forcing the needle through too-small beads can accelerate their demise. Take the time to test a few beads before anchoring thread to fabric and make sure you're using a small enough needle for the beads you've chosen.

Use sewing needles and sewing thread for hand basting and hand stitching seams.

Clockwise, starting at left: Three-ply hand-dyed needlework thread, size 3 perle cotton, size 8 perle cotton spools, size 5 perle cotton hanks, metallic fine braid.

Silk ribbon for embroidery is often sold on cards, but it also can be found at specialty shops in hanks or by the yard.

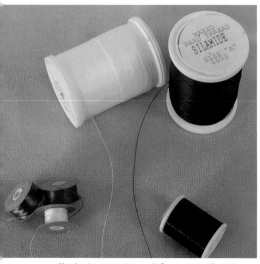

Clockwise, starting at left: Nymo, Silamide and Kevlar threads.

Embroidery Thread

Again, there are no rules. If you can get the thread through the eye of a needle and through the fabric, you can use it to make the decorative stitches. In general, choose a weight and color of thread that will show up against the fabric so your pretty needlework will stand out.

One thread type (I personally avoid) is six-strand embroidery floss; I much prefer the way perle (pearl) cotton looks for this type of embroidery work. I prefer sizes 5 and 8 (smaller numbers are larger threads) but occasionally use size 3, which almost looks like yarn. A fine-weight crochet or tatting thread works well too. Hand-dyed three-ply cotton needlework threads are lovely. The plies must be separated and used individually for most embroidery. Cotton threads hold up well with repeated passes through fabric, so you easily can use 24" to 30" lengths. And, since there aren't any rules here, if you like floss, go ahead and use it!

Metallic, Fine Braid, manufactured by Kreinik, is my favorite thread. (I prefer sizes 8 and 4). It is available in many beautiful colors. The thread is a little difficult to pull through fabrics, but using a slightly larger embroidery needle will help.

Rayon threads are lovely but require a little patience. They have a tendency to tangle.

Use 18" to 24" lengths of metallic and rayon thread or you'll spend too much time fighting knots and tangles.

Silk embroidery ribbons in sizes 4 mm, 7 mm and even 13 mm are great for working embroidery stitches and motifs. Use 12" to 18" lengths to avoid wearing out or fraying the ribbon from too many passes through the fabric.

Beading Thread

For many years I used Nymo, a readily available beading thread that comes in several sizes and many colors. It's a very good thread for stitching beads to fabric. I used it almost exclusively until I tried Silamide, a waxed thread, at the suggestion of a teacher in a bead embroidery class. Silamide also comes in several sizes and colors. I prefer size A and use it for all my beadwork.

You only need two colors of beading thread, white and black, for just about any bead-on-fabric situation. This concept has made my life so much simpler! I also love the color purple, so I use purple thread instead of black for almost everything. In instances where I'm sewing beads to a light-colored fabric background I use white Silamide.

I've found Kevlar thread to be impervious to the cutting and wearing that normally results when attaching bugle beads with sharp edges. It is great for stringing neckstraps that must endure heavy wear and tear.

Quilters' beeswax or Thread Heaven lubricant will help prevent thread knots from forming, especially with Nymo thread. Silamide doesn't tangle as much for me, so I don't use any thread lubricant with it.

Sewing Thread

A regular sewing thread is all you need for basting and assembling projects.

Occasionally, I use metallic sewing threads for delicate embroidery work (see the dragonfly wings on page 107). When using metallic thread, use 12" to 18" strands. The shorter strands prevent the thread from wearing out with the many repeated passes through the fabric.

Beads

The seed bead is a staple of crazy quilting (also called a rocaille). The most common size is 11/0; sizes 15/0, 8/0, 5/0 and 6/0 also are widely available. They are made of glass, come in many colors, cuts and finishes (such as matte or iris). All of them will work with crazy quilting, so collect what appeals to you. These beads come in a variety of containers, from small bags to large tubes, often measured by weight in grams. Larger quantities are sold strung on strands of thread which are bundled together (usually 12 strands) in hanks. Most of the projects in this book require a very small amount of seed beads, about a teaspoon or two. In projects where larger amounts are required, a quantity will be noted in the materials list.

Tubular **bugle beads** are a very common type of bead sold in a variety of colors, sizes and finishes. Be aware that some have sharp edges which can cut the thread. In the Woven Ribbon Sachet project on page 32, you will learn how to add beads to each end, minimizing the wear on your beading thread.

Another tubular bead, one that is extremely tiny, is the **micro tube** (see page 41, Nautilus Wall Hanging). They are very small, but that makes them ideal for projects where smooth curves are desirable. The only special tool you'll need is a small needle to fit through the bead.

Decorative beads are stated for all the other beads used in these projects. They come in a variety of sizes, colors, and shapes and can be glass, ceramic or semiprecious stones — technically, anything with a hole qualifies. Once you start looking, you'll find the choices are seemingly endless. Some of the staples I keep for crazy quilting are small teardrops (tims) daggers (fringe beads) and leaf beads.

If you have a friend who uses beads, trade portions of your stash. It is a great way for both of you to expand your inventory.

Note: The thread used in bead hanks to contain the beads is not intended for end use. Remove only the beads you need from the strand, leaving the rest intact for storing. Otherwise, store partially used strands in bags or other containers.

Bugle beads are sold in a variety of containers and sizes. Micro tubes (second from top) are generally sold on hanks.

Buttons and Charms

Buttons are a natural choice for crazy quilting, as are charms and anything else you can stitch down!

Trims and Fibers

Fancy trims and luxurious fibers are wonderful additions to crazy quilting and work extremely well with beaded accents. Again, a little yardage goes a long way. Keep an eye out for the ones that call to you and buy a yard here and there; soon you'll have a nice collection.

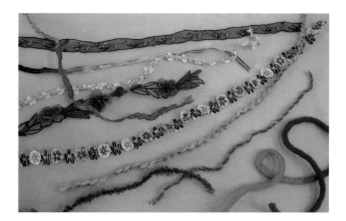

Clockwise from top: Some of my favorite tools: needle board for pressing velvet; quilters' pins with large heads; a rubber needle grabber; a tiny bead scoop.

Tools and Helpers

Thimbles

I have tried many times to wear a thimble and just don't care for them. If you are comfortable using a thimble, use it. I use small, round rubber disks called **"Needle Grabbers"** for embroidering and beading quilting projects, especially when using thick fibers or silk ribbon and stitching through several layers of fabric. You can find them in the sewing and quilting notions departments.

Needle Board

I use velvet quite often, so I've invested in a needle board for pressing it. This 5" x 13" bed of tiny dull needles lays right on my ironing board. The velvet goes pile-side down on the needles so you can press wrinkles out of the back of the velvet without crushing the pile. In lieu of a needle board, use a second piece of velvet and place the velvets pile-to-pile. Carefully press the first piece from the back, applying only enough pressure to remove the wrinkles, but not enough to flatten the velvet nap. Another option is a terry cloth towel. Place terry to pile, and press the velvet from the back. This last option is the least satisfactory, as sometimes the terry leaves its impression on the velvet.

Scissors

You will need sewing shears or scissors for cutting fabric. I highly recommend a pair of small scissors for cutting threads, although you could get by with just the sewing shears.

Iron and Ironing Board

You also will need an iron and ironing board.

Sewing Machine

A sewing machine will come in handy for assembling projects, but hand sewing will work fine.

Straight Pins

I recommend good quality pins with a large head so you easily can see them. It's easy for pins to get lost in all the embellishments of crazy quilting.

Embroidery Hoop

I don't use an embroidery hoop, but if it is something you are comfortable using, then it's not breaking any rule to do so. Prepare your motif patches so they will be large enough to hoop. Remove the crease caused by the hoop when finished.

Fabric Markers

A permanent fine-tip marker is ideal for transferring patterns to interfacing. An air-erasable marker is indispensable for transferring patterns onto light- and medium-colored fabric.

Light Source

Inexpensive light boxes are quite handy. If you don't have one, tape the pattern to a window and use daylight.

Ruler and/or Straight Edge

You'll need a fabric measuring tool and a straight edge for marking seam allowances on foundations.

Beading Workstation

There are all sorts of ways to keep your beads from getting away from you as you work, from flocked bead boards to a simple piece of felt. Small triangular bead dishes work well too. A tiny scoop is indispensable for picking up leftover beads and returning them to their containers.

Basic Techniques

Prep a Patch

You'll notice the patterns in this book are sometimes reversed (mirror image) from the finished project. Transfer these patterns to the non-adhesive side of fusible interfacing, then fuse the interfacing to the back of a fabric patch. In other cases, where it's better to have the pattern drawn right on the fabric, you'll still reinforce the patch with plain fusible interfacing.

The interfacing can extend to the edges of the patch without causing problems, but those edges may need to be turned under. I generally make the interfacing ½" smaller (all around) than the patch itself. This also helps determine where the seam allowance is and you can avoid stitching or beading into it. (This can cause problems during the assembly process.)

Follow the manufacturer's recommended instructions when fusing the interfacing to your fabric.

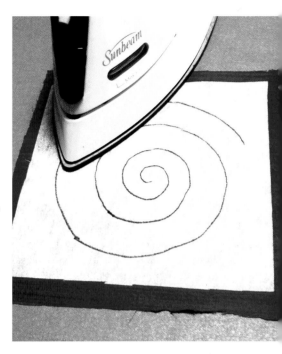

Transfer a Pattern

I've suggested three different ways to transfer patterns throughout the book.

1 Trace the pattern directly onto the non-adhesive side of fusible interfacing, then fuse to the back of the patch. Remember to use mirror-image patterns when using this method. The pattern will be on the back of your patch. Hold your work so you can see the back as you insert your needle. It sounds tricky, but it's pretty easy with a little practice.

2 Some projects will have the pattern on the front of the fabric. This method works with fabrics that are light enough in color to use with an air-erasable fabric marker. Trace the pattern onto tracing paper using a black fine-tip marker. Place the pattern onto a light box or tape to a window using daylight as your light source. Place the prepared patch on top of the pattern and retrace using an air-erasable marker.

3 Air-erasable markers will not show up on dark fabrics and some light-colored velvets. When the pattern needs to be on the front of the patch, follow Step 1 to get the pattern on the back of the patch, then baste on the traced line with sewing thread in a color that shows up against your fabric to get the design on the front. The basted design will show on the front of the patch.

• •

Note: Depending on how long you take to complete your stitching, the air-erase marked lines may disappear and it will be necessary to redraw them before you complete the stitching or beading.

• •

Stitching Basics
Knotting a Thread

It sounds a bit odd, but I use different knot methods to start my stitching and to end the stitching.

To start, thread a needle. Hold it with the thread end hanging down and your needle pointing straight up. With the index finger of the hand holding the needle, hold the thread end against the needle. Wrap the thread, just above your finger, around the needle four or five times. Holding the wraps against the needle, carefully pull the needle through, sliding the wraps past the eye and down to the end of the thread. You'll have a nice, neat knot. (It may take a little practice to learn this.) Then take the stitch up through the fabric, letting the knot rest snugly against the back, and begin stitching. This is the knot I use for my embroidery and bead stitching whenever I change threads.

To end the stitching, or knot-off, take three or four small stitches on top of each other at the back of the fabric and trim the thread, leaving an inch or so of thread tail.

Basting

Use sewing thread to make long, temporary running stitches (page 14) mark pattern lines or temporarily hold things together. For patterns, use a thread color that will contrast with your fabric. After the beadwork and embroidery are completed, carefully remove any basting stitches that are still visible.

Tack

This small, mostly invisible stitch is used to attach trims or similar accents to a quilt surface. Use a sewing or beading thread that blends in with the trim and fabric. Place stitches close together to hold the item securely to the fabric.

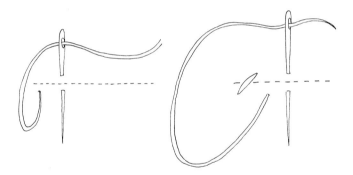

Whipstitch

An overhand stitch is used to hand sew two edges together, such as closing a portion of a seam which was left open for turning. Use a thread color to match the fabric and short, evenly-spaced stitches.

Silk Ribbon Embroidery

These stitches are made similar to thread embroidery, but there are a few special techniques for working with ribbon.

1 Press the ribbon to remove creases made by the packaging. Use short (12" to 18") lengths of ribbon. The ribbon will wear a little with each pass through the fabric.

2 Thread one end of the ribbon through the eye of a chenille or embroidery needle, leaving a short tail near the eye. Pierce the center of the tail, close to the end, and pull on the long end of the ribbon; this will lock the ribbon to the needle.

3 To knot the tail end of the ribbon, fold the ribbon over ¼" from the end. Pierce through both layers of ribbon at the tail

with needle. Slide needle through the layers, then slide the layers down the length of the ribbon, leaving a soft knot at the end.

4 Don't pull ribbon stitches as tight as you would with embroidered thread stitches; let them lie on top of the fabric. Try to keep the ribbon flat and untwisted for the most pleasing results.

5 Knot off ribbon at the back of your work by taking an extra stitch through the interfacing layer only, then weave the tail under a few existing stitches before cutting away from the needle.

Building a Crazy Quilt

The method I used to create the Sampler Square requires piecing the patches right onto a large piece of dense, low-loft quilt batting. For larger quilts, I suggest creating small blocks and joining them together with embroidered seams onto a large batting. See pages 109 through 119 for instructions on creating a small sampler.

Rather than baste or stitch the patches together first, pin them onto a foundation, folding the edges of the topmost patches under ½" where they overlap another patch. Embroider over each seam, right through the foundation, to hold the patches together. Work from the outside edges of the block inward to avoid getting poked by the pins. Basting is an option if you don't like the pin-and-embroider method.

Trims and fibers can be worked in as you embroider the seams, or after, depending on your preference. You can add beadwork as you go or embroider the seams first, then go back and add the beads.

Once the quilt top is finished (for me the hardest part is deciding exactly when it's "done") finish the quilt as you would any other quilt, adding a border and backing, if desired. Don't forget that the border is another great surface for additional beading!

Care and Cleaning of Beaded Crazy Quilts

This highly decorative style of crazy quilting with beads doesn't lend itself to the usual methods of laundering. Keep the finished piece free from dirt and spills. If soiling does occur, carefully spot clean with a damp cloth. If dust collects on a wall hanging or pillow, place a piece of nylon stocking over the end of a vacuum hose and vacuum the dust away. It is an easy way to clean without disturbing the delicate embellishments.

I've had success cleaning a crazy quilted garment using a dry-cleaning product made for use in household dryers. Commercial dry cleaning could remove the color from your beads and embellishments and permanently damage fibers, so I don't recommend it. My best advice is to treat your finished pieces with care to avoid soiling in the first place. Spot clean as necessary, and if a portion of the piece becomes damaged or soiled beyond repair, try adding new patches and beadwork to replace the damaged area.

The Projects

- Pillow Sachet with Spiral Motif
- Cell Phone Pouch with Raspberries
- Journal Cover
- Woven Ribbon Sachet
- Christmas Purse
- Nautilus Wall Hanging
- Gift Bag
- Sun Prints and Canister
- Eyeglass Pouch
- Strawberry Pocket Purse
- Doorknob Pouch with Grapes
- Grapes All Around Necklace
- Four Stamped Patches
    Filigree Heart
    Mutlicolored Leaf
    Double Heart
    Sun
- Bejeweled Vase Patch
- Featherstitch Patch
- Ribbons and Fibers Patch
- Beaded Lavender Sprigs Patch
- Silk Ribbon Flowers Patch
- Sampler Square

PILLOW SACHET WITH SPIRAL MOTIF

*One of the easiest
and most versatile
embroidery stitches is
the blanket stitch. Two
others that fall into
the easy-and-versatile
category are fly (or Y)
stitch and featherstitch.*

Prepare the Design

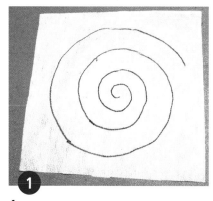

1 Using fabric marker, trace the pattern onto the non-adhesive side of interfacing.

2 Fuse interfacing to back of silk.

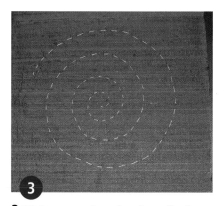

3 With sewing thread and needle, baste the design.

materials

- Spiral pattern (page 126)
- 6½" square fusible interfacing
- 7¼" square silk or other fabric
- 9" x 6¼" lining fabric
- 9" x 5¼" lining fabric
- (4) 9" lengths of 1½"-wide ribbon
- 6" x 18" quilt batting, folded into thirds (to make three layers)
- Size 11/0 seed beads: medium blue for spiral, light blue and dark blue for corners and frame
- Size 5/0 or 6/0 blue rocaille beads
- Short bugle beads: light blue and two shades of purple
- Permanent fabric marker
- Iron and ironing board
- Size 8 metallic Fine Braid embroidery thread
- Size 5 perle cotton
- Embroidery needle
- Beading needle
- Beading thread
- Sewing thread and needle
- Scraps of ribbon or fabric
- Scissors
- Ruler
- Optional: sewing machine

techniques

This project will teach you three basic embroidery stitches and simple beading techniques as you create a striking embellished block for a sachet filled with lavender buds…or save it to use in a larger crazy-patch project.

bead quantities

Bead quantities are less than one teaspoon/5 grams/500 beads for each type, unless otherwise noted. Colors are your choice. Thread quantities are less than a skein or spool, unless otherwise noted. Please read the information in Chapter 1 before starting your project.

Blanket Stitch the Spiral Pattern

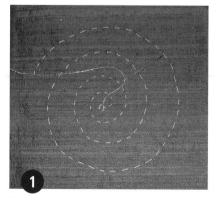

1 Using metallic thread and embroidery needle, start at center of design and make first blanket stitch (page 16).

2 Continue to blanket stitch around the entire spiral.

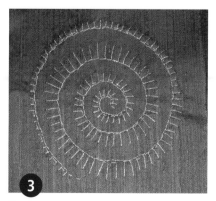

3 If you like, vary the length of the stitches (longer inside, shorter toward end).

EMBROIDERY STITCHES

Blanket Stitch

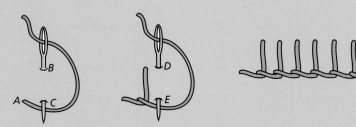

Bring needle up A, take back down at B and bring back up at C, keeping thread under the point of the needle. Pull thread snug to form stitch.

Start next stitch by taking needle down at D, up at E and down at F. Repeat for each stitch.

End stitches by coming up at D, cross over, and take back down right next to thread at bend.

Fly (or Y) Stitch

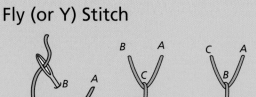

1st Stitch   *2nd Stitch*   *3rd Stitch*

Bring needle up A, take back down at B and bring back up at C, keeping thread under the point of the needle. Go back down at D. Pull thread snug to form stitch.

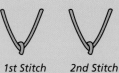

1st Stitch   *2nd Stitch*

For variation, change the distance between C and D, and/or between stitches.

Featherstitch

Bring needle up A, take back down at B and bring back up at C, keeping thread under the point of the needle. Go back down at D. Bring back up at E, go back down at F, up at G, down at H, up at I and so on.

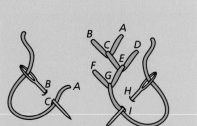

Variation

The featherstitch variation has two Y stitches going to one side or the other.

Add Beads

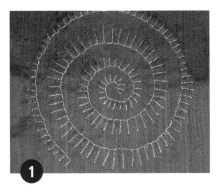

1 Using beading thread and needle, start at end (or center, if you prefer) and single stitch (page 17) one seed bead at end of each blanket stitch.

2 Continue adding seed beads around the entire spiral.

Add Corner Patches
Learn Fly and Featherstitches

1 Pin scraps of fabric or ribbon to corners.

2 Using perle cotton and featherstitch or fly-stitch (page 16) embroider the patch edges. Trim patches to make block square.

3 Stitch seed beads to embellish embroidery on corner patches, using single stitch or bead clusters (page 19) as desired.

4 Pin 9" pieces of ribbon around sides of patch, overlapping ribbon ⅜" onto patch and overlapping ribbon ends, log cabin style, as shown.

BEAD STITCHES

Anchor thread by knotting or take several stitches in the same place at the back of the fabric.

Use single- or double-strand beading thread and beading needle small enough to pass through the smallest beads selected for your project.

Single Stitch

Side view
Single stitch

Much like sewing on a button, bring needle up from back of fabric, through bead, and back down through fabric; pull thread snug to remove slack. Move needle at back of fabric to next bead position and repeat.

Assemble

1 Turn under ¼" hem on one long edge of lining panel and stitch down.

2 Press under the long edge of second lining panel. Overlap panels at center (pressed edge onto hemmed edge) right-side down. Adjust width of lining overlap and make the same overall size as patch.

3 Pin lining to patch, right sides together, and stitch around all sides using ⅜" seam allowance. Clip corners.

4 Turn right-side out through opening in lining.

5 Stitch ribbon edges to patch through all layers, including lining, to create a flange around the pillow. Use bead stitching (or embroidery stitching, if desired) to create the bead stitching as shown in the finished photo. Single stitch alternating short bugles and size 11/0 seeds across the top seam. Lazy daisy stitch (page 19) groups of three seeds along right edge. Single stitch alternating short bugles across bottom edge, and stitch two bead stacks (page 19) up the left edge. Be sure to extend stitching to outer corners.

6 Stuff pillow with three layers of batting and whipstitch the lining closed.

BEAD STITCHES

Bead Clusters

Any number of beads can be used to make a cluster, but it generally works best with an odd number less than 10.

Three-Bead Cluster

Bring needle up through fabric at A. Pick up two beads and take needle down at B. Come back up at C picking up one bead and go down at D, keeping the beads as close together as possible.

Top view

Another way to stitch a three-bead cluster is to bring needle up at A, pick up two beads and go down at B (same as above). Come back up between the beads at C or D (C will take needle across thread in previous stitch; D doesn't) and pick up third bead. Go back down at E, again keeping beads as close together as possible.

Method 2
Top view

Five-Bead Cluster

Bring needle up through fabric and pick up five beads. Slide beads to fabric and take needle back through same hole or right next to it. Do nothing further and the end of the cluster will stand up slightly off the fabric.

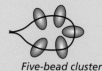

Five-bead cluster

Top view

If you want the cluster to lay flat, come back up beneath center bead in the loop, go through that bead only, and stitch back through fabric close to or in same hole you came up through.

Five-bead cluster option
Step 1 Same as above

Step 2

Lazy Stitch

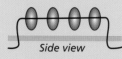

Side view

Bring needle up through fabric, pick up several seed beads and go back through fabric near last bead on thread. At back of fabric, move needle to next position and repeat, picking up the same or different number of beads.

Bead Stacks

Side view

Take needle through one or more beads, ending with a seed bead to serve as a stop bead, which will hold the bead(s) below it in place. Take needle back through all beads except stop bead and fabric. Pull thread snug to remove slack before proceeding to next bead stack.

CELL PHONE POUCH WITH RASPBERRIES

The pretty little berries are quite easy to stitch and they make any project look very elegant. Since I discovered the charm of these little berry jewels, I include them on every crazy quilt project I create.

Prepare the Pouch

1 Trace pattern from page 121 onto non-adhesive side of interfacing and cut out. Cut remaining fabric pieces from patterns as directed.

2 Fuse shapes to wrong side of velvet. Trim velvet shapes, adding ½" seam allowance on all sides.

3 Place velvet shapes, wrong sides down, on remaining interfacing or foundation. Turn under curved edge of uppermost velvet shape and pin through all layers.

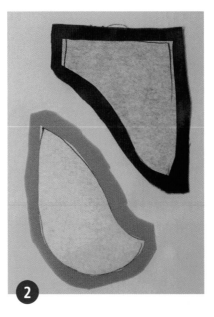

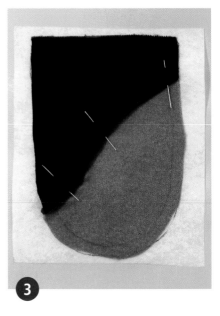

materials

- Patterns (pages 121 and 122)
- 4½" x 5½" fusible interfacing
- 4½" x 5½" non-fusible interfacing or other foundation
- Lavender and blue velvet fabric, each piece 4½" x 5½"
- 4½" x 5½" fabric (pouch back)
- 4½" x 11" fabric (lining)
- Sizes 5 and 8 green perle cotton (stems and leaves)
- 2 shades size 11/0 magenta and/or purple seed beads (berries)
- 4 mm dark blue cube beads
- 2 teaspoons size 11/0 dark blue seed beads
- 1 teaspoon size 10/0 dark blue charlottes
- 8 dark blue 8 mm pearls
- Size 6/0 magenta seeds
- 2 flower-shaped beads for strap
- Permanent fabric marker
- Beading needle
- Beading thread
- Embroidery needle
- Sewing thread and needle
- Iron and ironing board
- Scissors
- Ruler or tape measure
- Optional: sewing machine

techniques

Learn one of my favorite embroidery stitches, the maidenhair, plus two of the easiest and most useful stitches, the lazy daisy and stem stitch. Besides learning how to make the beaded berries, this project will have you stringing beads to make a neck strap and teach you how to make the pretty picot edging around the sides of the pouch.

bead quantities

Bead quantities are less than one teaspoon/5 grams/500 beads for each type, unless otherwise noted. Colors are your choice. Thread quantities are less than a skein or spool, unless otherwise noted. Please read the information in Chapter 1 before starting your project.

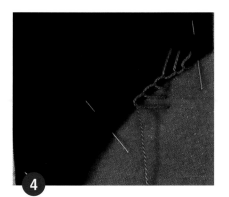

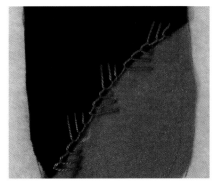

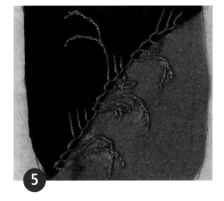

The second maidenhair points in the opposite direction from the first.

Maidenhair stitching completed.

4 Using size 5 perle cotton and embroidery needle, stitch along velvet seam using maidenhair stitch (page 22). Take care to go through all layers of fabric, including foundation. Do not stitch into seam allowances. Make sure folded edge of upper piece of velvet remains turned under. Complete the stitching to hold it in place.

5 Using size 5 perle cotton, stem stitch (page 22) out from the ends of a few maidenhair stitches into both velvet panels. Add a few lazy daisy stitches (page 22) for leaves.

21

EMBROIDERY STITCHES

Maidenhair Stitch

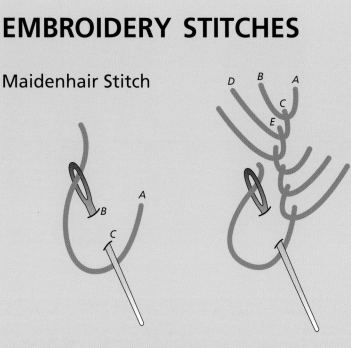

This is a variation of the featherstitch (page 16). Bring needle up at A and take down at B. Bring back up at C, keeping thread beneath needle. Go back down at D, and back up at E. Make three stitches at one side of row, each slightly longer than the last. Then do three similar stitches pointing in the opposite direction. Work down the row, aligning stitches vertically.

Stem Stitch

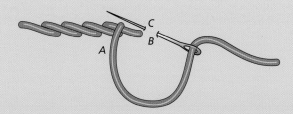

Optional: Mark guideline on fabric (if using dark velvet, make a basting stitch using light-colored sewing thread). Bring needle up at A and hold thread down with thumb of non-stitching hand. Take back down at B and bring back up at C, midway between A and B. Repeat, keeping stitches close together to form a continuous line.

Lazy Daisy Stitch

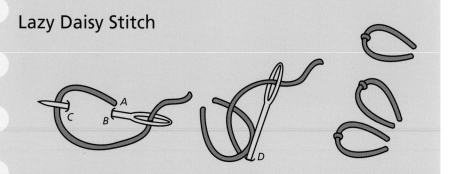

Bring needle up at A. Go back down at B, right next to A. Come back up at C, keeping thread loop under needle. Pull up to make a small loop, but not too tight. Take needle back down at D to hold end of loop in place against fabric.

Bead Raspberries

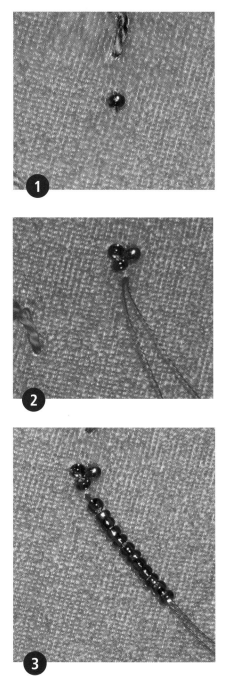

1 Using doubled beading thread and needle, stitch one size 11/0 purple bead near the end of a stem stitch.

2 Stitch two more beads in place, touching the first one. Bring needle back out through fabric near one of the beads.

3 Pick up 12 more beads and slide towards fabric.

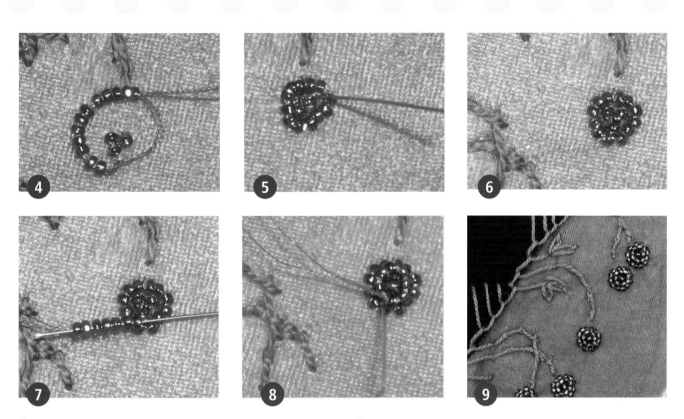

4 Take needle back through all beads, beginning with first one strung. Gently pull up slack in thread so beads begin to form a ring.

5 Pull thread snug, but not overly tight, forming a ring around center beads. Take needle down through fabric near bead ring. Couch (page 24) ring to fabric at two or three places. Bring needle back up through fabric in center of bead ring.

6 Stitch a single bead in center of cluster, letting it sit right on top of the original beads. Bring needle back up through fabric between ring and center beads.

7 Pick up eight more beads and slide towards berry. Take needle back through several beads strung in this step and gently pull up slack to form a second bead ring around single bead added in last step. This new ring will rest on top of the original ring.

8 Snug ring and take needle back into fabric between new ring and original ring. Carefully couch to fabric in one or two places, hiding stitches between large ring and berry center.

9 Repeat Steps 1 through 8 to create additional purple berries on lavender velvet panel. Switch to magenta beads to make berries on blue velvet panel.

10 Complete the berries: Use size 8 perle cotton and stitch five lazy daisy stitches (page 22) at base of each berry where it joins its stem. Add more lazy daisy stitches at the end of each maidenhair stitch.

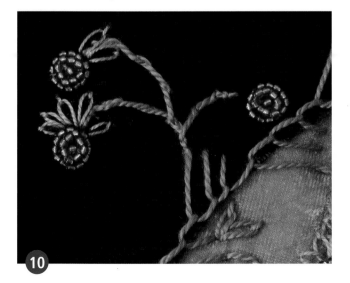

Assemble

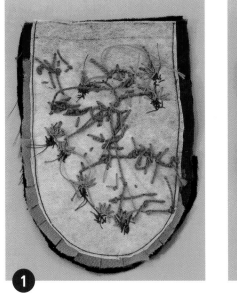

1 Stitch pouch front and back at sides and bottom, right sides together, using ½" seam allowance. Carefully cut excess interfacing foundation away from back of velvet. Clip curves of stitched pouch. Turn right-side out.

2 With right sides together, stitch the lining sides and bottom, leaving 2" opening at one side. Clip curves, but do not turn.

3 Place pouch inside of lining, right sides together, and stitch around top edge using ¼" seam allowance.

4 Turn right-side out through opening in lining. Stitch lining closed and tuck inside of pouch.

BEAD STITCHES

Couching

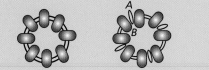

Top view

This stitch is used in embroidery as well as beading. Bring the needle up at A, just outside the ring of beads stitched. Take needle across the thread forming the ring and down inside the ring. To couch a straight row of beads, bring the needle up at one side of the thread within the row, across, and down on the other side.

Beadwork

Picot Edge

1 Anchor doubled beading thread at inside top edge of pouch. Bring needle out through seam of pouch and pick up five size 11/0 blue seed beads. (See picot edge diagram.)

2 Slide beads to fabric and take needle back down a short distance away, causing the beads to form an arc. It is not necessary to take the needle to the inside of the pouch, just catch some threads near the outside seam. Take up slack in thread, then bring needle back out through the last bead stitched and pick up two seeds, one cube and one seed.

3 Take needle back through cube and two seeds, pick up two seed beads and make stitch in fabric a short distance from last stitch.

4 Bring needle back out through last bead stitched. Pick up four size 11/0 seeds, and stitch to fabric. Repeat sequence all around bag to make picot edging.

Picot Edge

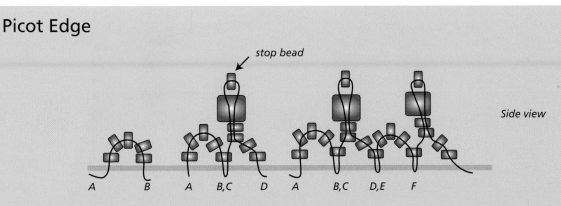

stop bead

Side view

A   B   A   B,C   D   A   B,C   D,E   F

Bring needle up at A, pick up five beads and take down at B, causing the beads to arch rather than lay flat against the fabric. Come back up at C (right next to B) and through last bead stitched. Pick up two seeds, one cube and one seed (stop bead). Go back through cube and two seeds, pick up two more seeds and back into fabric at D. Begin the same sequence again, coming up at E and through last bead stitched. Pick up four seeds and go down at F. Repeat the sequence around the entire edge of your project.

Strap

Finished length is 36"; adjust for a shorter or longer strap.

1 Anchor 48" beading thread (8 feet doubled) to inside top of pouch. Alternate segments of 10 size 11/0 seeds and eight size 10/0 charlottes, placing a cube, pearl, flower or size 6/0 bead between each segment. String to approximately 18" (or the halfway mark for your size) and place on a distinctive bead to serve as your marker. If you want your strap to be symmetrical, repeat the stringing order in reverse to complete the second half. Anchor to opposite side of pouch top and trim thread tails.

2 Anchor a new 48" doubled thread to pouch top and string the second set of size 10/0 and 11/0 bead segments parallel to the first, taking the needle through existing cubes, pearls, flowers and size 6/0 beads as you go. Secure at opposite end of pouch.

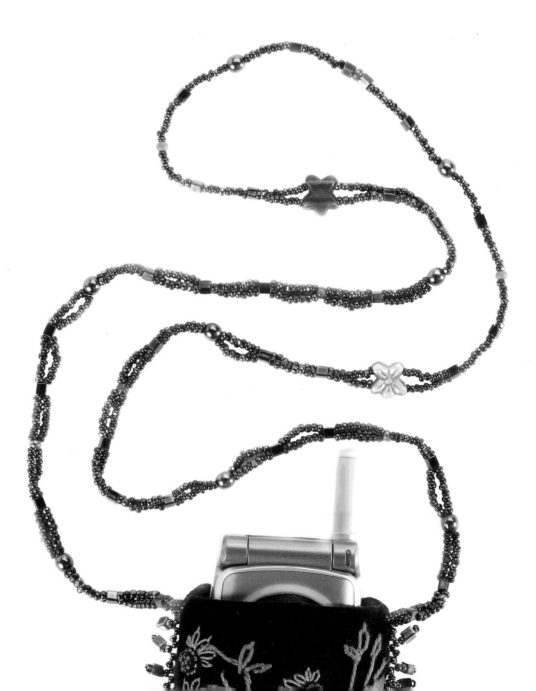

JOURNAL COVER

I love silk ribbon embroidery and admire those who have practiced and enhanced their skills to make perfect and precise stitches. I tend to be less concerned with the precision of each stitch. Its unique overall effect produces a gorgeous embroidered creation. If you've been discouraged by "old-school" silk ribbon techniques, give this simpler approach a try.

materials

- Pattern (page 123)
- 6" x 8½" journal
- 2 pieces 6½" x 8½" fusible interfacing
- 2 pieces 12" x 8½" fusible interfacing
- 2 pieces 17" x 9½" fabric (cover)
- 5 pink and purple 7"-wide x 4"-long fabrics or wide ribbon (patches)
- 5 pieces 4 mm silk ribbon 18" to 36" long: five shades of pink and/or purple (such as, magenta, hot pink, orchid, lavender, periwinkle, dark lilac)
- Size 8 perle cotton in shades of pink and purple
- 2 triangle-shaped focal beads
- 1 teaspoon purple bugle beads
- Size 11/0 pink seed beads
- Size 6/0 purple seed beads
- 1 teaspoon size 11/0 lavender beads (edging)
- Beading needle
- Beading thread
- Embroidery needle
- Sewing thread and needle
- Iron and ironing board
- Scissors
- Ruler or tape measure
- Optional: Sewing machine

techniques

While the predominant element of this journal cover is the silk ribbon stitching, there are plenty of other details that make this a one-of-a-kind book cover. Learn a fly stitch variation, how to embroider over seams to secure the edges, useful beading techniques and the all-important silk ribbon stitch. Open all kinds of creative doors for your needlework!

bead quantities

Bead quantities are less than one teaspoon/5 grams/500 beads for each type, unless otherwise noted. Colors are your choice. Thread quantities are less than a skein or spool, unless otherwise noted. Please read the information in Chapter 1 before starting your project.

Prepare the Cover

1 Trace pattern from page 123 onto non-adhesive side of smaller fusible interfacing for foundation. Mark seam allowance on three sides.

2 Fuse fabrics and wide ribbon to foundation, turn under raw edges of fabric, if necessary. Hand or machine baste around edges using ½" seam allowance.

3 Embroider edges of pieced patches using perle cotton and fly stitch variations (page 29).

4 Hand baste motif design using contrasting sewing thread.

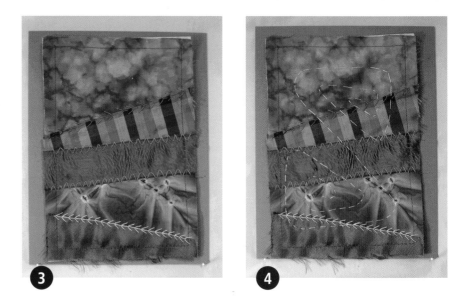

Silk Ribbon Embroidery

Tip: For best-looking results, press silk ribbon with iron on low silk setting, removing creases prior to stitching. Use 18" to 24" lengths of silk ribbon and embroidery needle to fly stitch design (page 29). Start at center of one spiral and work along pattern line. Switch colors of ribbon as you work, graduating from light pinks/purples to dark pinks/purples. Construct stitches in the same way as you would using embroidery thread, but don't pull ribbon as snug as you pull thread. Allow ribbon to lay on top of fabric, keeping it as flat as possible.

EMBROIDERY STITCHES

See basic fly stitch, page 16.

Fly Stitch Variations

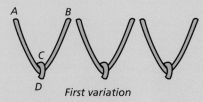

First variation

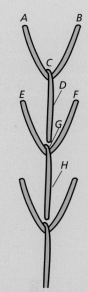

Work these stitches side by side horizontally. Bring needle up at A, take back down at B and bring back up at C, keeping thread under the point of the needle. Go back down at D. Pull thread snug to form stitch. Start second stitch by bringing thread from back, next to or in same hole as B from previous stitch.

Make a longer stitch from C to D than for the basic fly stitch. To start next stitch, bring needle back up at E, which is at a point midway between C and D from first stitch. Take needle down at F, bring up at G, right next to or in same hole as D, and down at H. The finished row will look continuous with no gaps between the vertical portions of stitches.

Second variation

SILK RIBBON STITCHES

See basic fly stitch, page 16.

Fly Stitch

Work this stitch just like an embroidered fly stitch. For this project, make the stitches as directed above for the second embroidered fly stitch variation, where the vertical portions of the stitches connect without any gaps between the end of one and beginning of the next. Bring needle up at A, take back down at B and bring back up at C, keeping ribbon under the point of the needle and as flat as possible. Go back down at D. Use smaller stitches in the tighter areas of the motif to get around the tight curves.

Beadwork

1 Using doubled beading thread in needle, stitch triangle focal bead (see diagram) at center of each spiral. Add more beads around and onto ribbon embroidery using single and bead stack techniques (page 19).

2 Add beads to fly-stitched embroidery along seam edges.

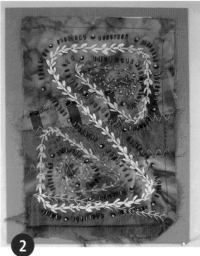

BEAD STITCHES

Focal Bead

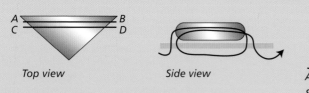

Top view   Side view

Although a triangular-shaped bead is shown here, this would work with any somewhat flat, large bead. Bring needle up at A, right next to the bead. Take thread through hole and down at B, right next to bead. Bring needle back up at C, go through bead again, and down at D. For heavy beads, repeat several times to reinforce the threads and stabilize the bead.

Edging

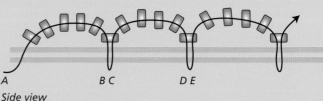

Side view

Bring needle up at A, string on six beads, go down at B catching journal fabric next to edge of appliqué. Bring needle up at C through edge of appliqué (right next to B) and back through last bead stitched. Pick up five beads and take needle down at D into journal cover fabric, back up at E through edge of appliqué and through last bead stitched. Pick up five more beads and repeat sequence.

Assemble Front Cover

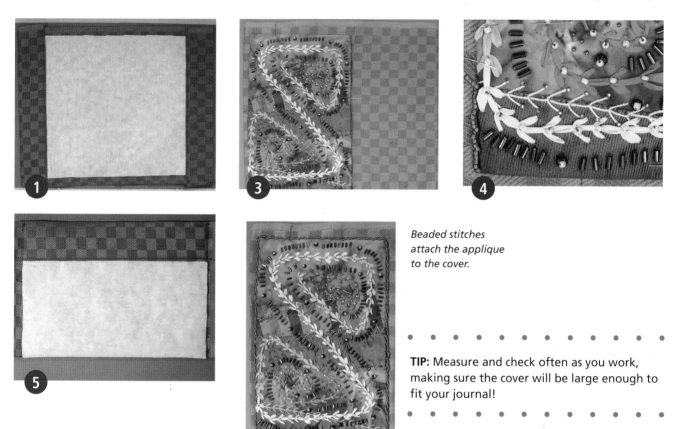

Beaded stitches attach the applique to the cover.

TIP: Measure and check often as you work, making sure the cover will be large enough to fit your journal!

1 Reinforce journal fabric cover by fusing large interfacing panel to center of wrong side.

2 Fold 17" side edges under ½" and press. Fold each side, wrong sides together, meeting edge of interfacing. Press. Hem folded edges, stitching through all fabric layers. Fold cover in half and press to mark center.

3 Fold edges of appliqué under ½" along all four sides and press. Pin to left front of cover. Adjust, making sure the appliqué fits within the seam allowances at top and bottom and within outside front of cover from side to side.

4 Use bead edging (page 30) to secure appliqué to cover. Starting at bottom left corner, anchor doubled beading thread at back of cover and bring out of fabric, catching the appliqué corner. Pick up six lavender beads and move needle approximately ⅜" from beginning of stitch, just far enough to allow the beads to lay flat or nearly flat. With needle, catch a few threads of the journal fabric and the edge of the appliqué. Bring needle back up through last bead stitched and pick up five more beads for next stitch. Continue all around appliqué to attach it to the journal cover.

5 Fold cover along pressed line, wrong sides together. Stitch cover front to back along bottom and top edges using ¼" seam allowance.

Assemble Back Cover

Assemble as for front cover, omitting steps pertaining to appliqué. Slide fabric covers over journal's covers, leaving spine exposed.

WOVEN RIBBON SACHET

As a collector of ribbons and fibers, I always seem to have short pieces left over from projects. Here's a way to use them up! You might have learned to weave strips of paper in elementary school art class — use that basic principle to create the top of this sachet or a patch for your crazy quilt projects.

Weave

1 Place low-tack masking tape around edges of organza to keep them from raveling. Place a strip of double-sided tape across top edge right on top of the masking tape.

2 Lay strips of assorted ribbons and fibers across the organza. Press one end onto the top of tape to hold in place. Don't cover the organza from edge to edge — keep strips an inch or so from each side.

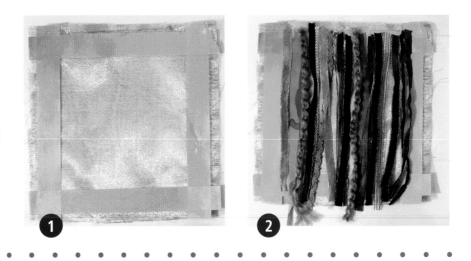

Tip: Test tape for ease of removal. If it doesn't easily come away from the organza, condition it by placing against your shirt sleeve and lifting several times to diffuse the strength of the adhesive.

materials

- 6" square green organza (front)
- 6" x 9" coordinating color organza (back)
- 1 yd. 1½"-wide ribbon for edging
- Assorted ribbons and fibers up to ⅜" wide x 6" long (weaving)
- Size 11/0 seed beads: purple, green, teal
- Small green cube beads
- Size 6/0 green seed beads
- Green niblets (flat rectangular) beads
- 8 long-twisted green bugle beads
- Focal bead or button (center of motif)
- 8 long green bugle beads
- Lavender buds or other sachet filling
- Metallic embroidery thread
- Beading needle
- Beading thread
- Embroidery needle
- Sewing needle and thread
- Low-tack masking tape
- Double-sided tape
- Scissors
- Ruler or tape measure
- Optional: sewing machine

techniques

Dive into your scrap bag and round up fibers, yarns and ribbons of varying widths — even those skinny scraps of fabric can be used here. Learn this easy way to weave them into a special fabric and hold it all together with beaded stitches.

bead quantities

Bead quantities are less than one teaspoon/5 grams/500 beads for each type, unless otherwise noted. Colors are your choice. Thread quantities are less than a skein or spool, unless otherwise noted. Please read the information in Chapter 1 before starting your project.

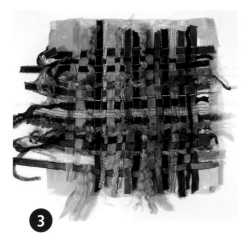

3 Place strips of double-sided tape along side edges on top of the masking tape to hold horizontal ribbons and fibers as you weave them through the vertical strips. To weave, simply lift every other vertical strip and slide the horizontal strip beneath them. Work horizontal strip into a straight position. With the next horizontal strip, place it beneath the opposite vertical strips as before. After each horizontal strip is added, place your hand over the ends of vertical strips at bottom and nudge the strip into place. A pin or needle can be useful to coax strips into position. Try to keep the strips close together and straight across the weaving in both directions. This will take some effort. Be patient, and don't try to do this step in 5 minutes! Trim excess ends from woven strips.

Add the Beads

1 Single stitch a variety of seed beads along the four outside ribbon/fiber strips to hold them in place. Remove the tape very carefully. (Try to avoid stitching through the tape; let the ends of the fibers and ribbons remain loose.) Continue to stitch a few more beads around the outermost areas of the weaving.

2 Stitch a focal bead or button (page 30) to the center of the motif, then stitch long bugle beads (page 35) radiating around the focal bead. Randomly place and stitch beads around the remaining areas of the weaving using single stitch (page 17) and lazy stitch (page 19) for decoration. This will secure the weaving to the organza

3 Cut the rectangle of backing organza in half. Fold and press under a narrow hem where the edges overlap at the center. Pin backing pieces to sachet top, right sides together, folding ends of woven strips out of the way of the ¼" seam allowance. Stitch all around, being careful not to catch ends of woven strips.

Assemble

1 Clip corners.

2 Turn right-side out.

3 Cut 1½"-wide ribbon into four equal 9" pieces and arrange around the edges of the sachet. Overlap onto body of sachet front ⅛" between organza and ends of woven strips. Pin in place.

4 Blanket stitch (page 16) edge of ribbon to sachet using short stitches and taking care not to catch ends of woven strips.

5 Fold overlapped ribbon corners at 45-degree angles and fly stitch (page 16) to finish.

6 Trim excess ribbon at back of corners. Fill pouch with sachet filling and whipstitch (page 10) the opening closed.

BEAD STITCHES

Bugle Beads

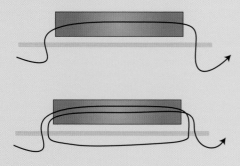

First Method

Often these beads have sharp edges that can cut through thread with wear. There are a couple of things you can do to help prevent this. First, you can make two or three passes through the bead, thus using several strands of thread to hold the bead to the fabric, making it less likely that the bead will wear through all the strands.

Second Method

The second method is to string a seed bead at one or both ends of the bugle, so the thread will not be in direct contact with the edge of the bugle itself. For this project, I chose the first method, since sachets don't tend to get a lot of wear and tear. (At the end of each bugle, stitch a small teardrop bead in place for decoration only.)

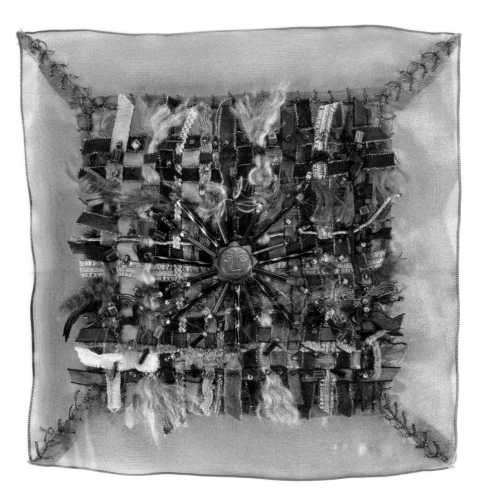

CHRISTMAS PURSE

Being able to use my inkjet printer to create my own fabric has vastly changed the way I create crazy quilt motifs! For nearly three decades I've been loving, collecting and using clip art in my profession (graphic design) and now, I have another surface to which to apply all those lovely images.

Fabric Printing

1 Using your computer and scanner, scan the wreath image on page 128, and place it on a document page. Scale it up or down, if desired, or leave as is to print a 4¼" square image. Size a face image of your choice (photo or clip art) to fit in 1¾" diameter circle.

2 Get the best usage from your inkjet-printable fabric. Add other images to your sheet, such as those from other projects in this book. Test print a piece of paper first, and if satisfactory, print onto the fabric.

3 Use the electric rhinestone applicator to affix red nailheads to the wreath wherever there are red berries in the image. Follow the instructions included with the appliance.

materials

- Wreath image, page 128
- Clip art image of girl's face or photo of your choice sized to 1¾" diameter
- 1⅞" half-ball cover button
- 6½" x 7" fusible interfacing
- 7½" x 15" green fabric (purse)
- 7½" x 15" fabric (lining)
- 5¼" x 5¼" fabric (pocket lining)
- 3¾" square quilt batting, plus small amount for button
- 20" sheer green 1½"-wide wired ribbon
- 48" green cording (strap)
- 30 red 6 mm hot-fix round metal nailheads
- Size 11/0 clear and silver-lined hex-cut seed beads
- Size 11/0 iridescent white seed beads
- Size 15/0 green seed beads
- 4 mm red diamond-shaped Swarovski crystals
- Computer with scanner and inkjet printer
- Inkjet-printable fabric
- Double-sided tape
- Electric rhinestone applicator
- Beading needle
- White beading thread
- Embroidery needle
- Sewing thread and needle
- Iron and ironing board
- Scissors
- Ruler or tape measure
- Optional: sewing machine

techniques

When printing on inkjet fabric, make the most of your fabric sheet. Fill the page with usable images so none of the fabric goes to waste. Small images are perfect to cover button blanks, which in turn make a great vehicle for bead netting. You'll also use a rhinestone setter to hot-fix embellishments to an image and learn how to frame an image using an easy scrunched ribbon technique.

bead quantities

Bead quantities are less than one teaspoon/5 grams/500 beads for each type, unless otherwise noted. Colors are your choice. Thread quantities are less than a skein or spool, unless otherwise noted. Please read the information in Chapter 1 before starting your project.

Button

1 Using template provided with cover button, trace circle approximately twice as large as button diameter around face image, keeping image centered. Cut a circle of batting to diameter of button.

2 Use double-sided tape to adhere batting to button and cover button with fabric following manufacturer's directions.

3 Anchor single strand of beading thread close to the back edge of button fabric.

4 Pick up five clear seed beads; slide up to edge of button. Take stitch into button fabric, ¼" away from first stitch. The distance needs to be small enough so the beads will arch away from button edge. Bring needle back up through last bead stitched, pick up four beads and make the next stitch. Repeat around perimeter of button.

5 To complete last stitch, pick up three beads and take needle through first bead of first stitch. Anchor thread to fabric toward back of button behind beading.

6 Bring needle back up through three beads in first row of stitching. Pick up the following beads: three white, one green, one clear and one silver. Go back through clear and green beads, pick up three more white beads, and take needle through center bead of next loop of first row.

7 Work second row of beading all around button. This beading technique is called netting (page 39).

8 Sew wreath square to pocket lining with right sides together and using ¼" seam allowance around sides and top. Clip corners and turn right-side out. Insert square of quilt batting between fabric layers and whipstitch (page 10) opening closed.

9 Stitch button to center of pocket through all layers of fabric.

Covered button with fabric image.

BEAD STITCHES

Bead Netting

Side views

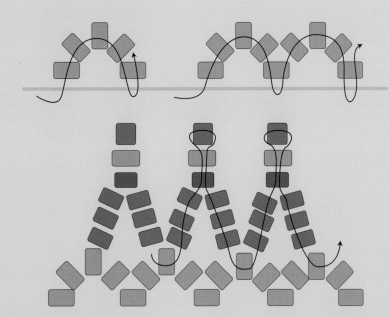

Anchor beading thread to fabric, hiding knot at back. Pick up an uneven number of seed beads (I used five). Stitch back into fabric a short distance from first stitch to make the beads arch away from fabric. Bring needle back up through last bead stitched and pick up four beads (one less than you started with, if you are making loops all the same size). Continue to work around button. For the last stitch, pick up three beads and take needle back through first bead in row. Anchor thread at back of fabric.

For second row of netting, bring needle out through beads and emerge at center bead in one of the loops. Pick up more beads (in this case, three size 11/0 beads, one size 15/0 and two size 11/0 beads). The last bead is the stop bead, go back through the others until you emerge from the size 15/0. Pick up three more size 11/0 beads and take needle through center bead of next loop in first row.

You could keep adding rows and rows for a very elaborate netting! For this project, we will make two rows to complete the button.

Assemble

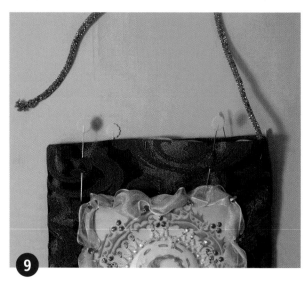

3 Pin pocket to purse front.

4 Hand sew pocket to purse front along sides and bottom.

5 Anchor double strand of beading thread inside purse at lower right pocket corner. Pinch sheer ribbon 1" from end, and position at bottom of right corner of pocket. Bring needle through ribbon at pinch. Pick up a clear or silver seed bead, red crystal, seed bead and make stitch back through ribbon pinch to anchor it to the purse front.

6 Slide needle approximately 1" to left, bring through fabric and a second ribbon pinch. Repeat process to stitch a ribbon frame around the pocket. At top of pocket, stitch ribbon to pocket edge (not to purse itself). At bottom right corner, fold and tuck ribbon ends under and stitch down with an invisible stitch.

7 Fold purse lining in half with right sides together. Stitch sides using ½" seam allowance. Clip corners.

8 Fold top edge under ¾" and press.

9 Place and pin lining inside purse, adjusting top edges to match. Knot ends of cord for strap and insert between purse and lining at side seams. Stitch around top of purse by hand or machine.

1 Fold purse fabric in half and press crease at fold. Press under ½" on both short edges. Fuse 6½" x 7" interfacing panel to center of purse front on wrong side (reinforcement).

2 Stitch purse sides with right sides together. Clip corners. Turn right-side out.

NAUTILUS WALL HANGING

I admired my beautiful nautilus shell sitting on a shelf for years, until one day I decided to scan it and use it as a base for a digital illustration. The rest is, as they say, history…or at least the way this project came about!

materials

- Nautilus image, page 128
- Scrollwork pattern, page 124
- Nautilus outline pattern, page 126
- 8½" x 11" inkjet-printable fabric (half sheet will be used)
- 10" x 6½" silk panel
- 4½" x 6" fusible interfacing
- Size 8 purple metallic Fine Braid embroidery thread
- 2 to 3 strands of 2 mm clear silver-lined micro-tube beads
- Size 15/0 purple seed beads
- Size 15 beading needle
- Beading thread in a dark and light color
- Fine-tip black permanent fabric
- Air-erasable fabric marker
- 6" x 8" tracing or tissue paper
- Scissors
- Embroidery needle
- Iron and ironing board
- Decorative hanging hardware or dowel and cord (hanging)
- Computer and ink jet printer
- Ruler or tape measure

techniques

At a bead show, I stumbled across the tiniest bugle beads one could imagine! They shimmered and draped beautifully, strung and bundled in the most delicate hanks. The vendor called them "waterfall beads." (I've since learned they are more commonly called micro-tubes. A special size 15 beading needle is required. The hanging hardware is another of those accidental "finds." It was in my stash for years before I realized it was the perfect size for this project.

bead quantities

Bead quantities are less than one teaspoon/5 grams/500 beads for each type, unless otherwise noted. Colors are your choice. Thread quantities are less than a skein or spool, unless otherwise noted. Please read the information in Chapter 1 before starting your project.

Print on Fabric

1 Using your computer, scan the nautilus image (page 128) and place it on a document page. Place the image on only one half of the page. Test print a piece of paper first, and if satisfactory, print onto fabric. Cut fabric in half and save un-printed piece for another project (or fill page with something else and print the whole sheet).

Appliqué Technique

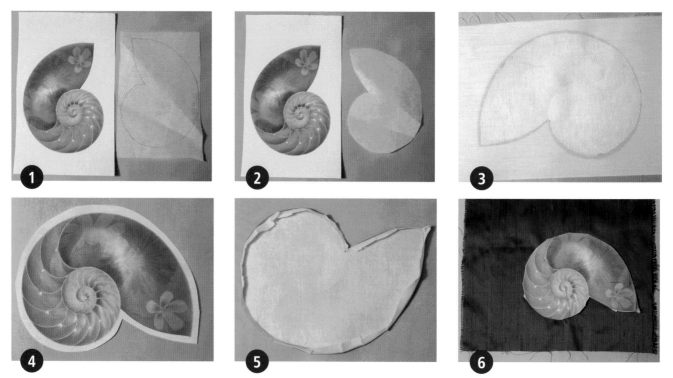

1 Trace nautilus outline onto non-adhesive side of interfacing.

2 Cut out interfacing shape.

3 Fuse interfacing shape to wrong side of printed nautilus.

4 Cut out nautilus shape, adding ⅜" all around.

5 Clip curves and notch valley of white fabric margin around nautilus imprint. Press margin to back of shape.

6 Pin nautilus appliqué to silk panel approximately 1¼" from bottom edge and centered from side to side.

BEAD STITCHES

Beaded Backstitch

Side view

For a continuous row or line of beads, bring thread up from back of fabric, pick up six beads and go back into fabric near last bead, snugging the beads together. The beads should lay flat and close together with no gaps or thread showing. Bring needle back up between fourth and fifth stitched beads and go through the last two beads again, emerging from the last stitched bead. Pick up six beads, go back into fabric near end bead and come back up between third and second bead from stitched end. Go through last two stitched beads and pick up six beads. Repeat sequence to create a continuous row.

This is a versatile technique, as you can create straight or curved lines with ease. If a row ends up a little wobbly, run the thread back through all the beads and they will magically line up smoothly.

Bead the Appliqué

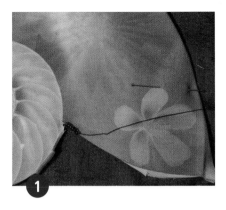

A few inches of beaded backstitch completed.

Beaded backstitch outlines the appliqué as well as attaching it to the foundation panel.

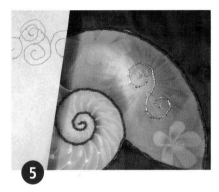

1 Starting at valley of nautilus appliqué, anchor single strand of dark-colored beading thread at back of silk and bring needle up through applique, close to edge. Pick up six purple seed beads to make your first beaded backstitch (see diagram). Continue to backstitch around the entire perimeter of the appliqué, adding six beads per stitch.

2 When you reach the starting point at the valley, continue the beaded backstitch around the spiral inside the nautilus (see finished photo). Anchor beading thread at back of silk and trim tails.

3 Trace the scrollwork design onto tracing or tissue paper. Place over appliqué and pin at one corner, so you can fold it out of the way, without moving it out of position.

4 Use the scrollwork design as a guide. With an air-erasable fabric marker, draw an S-shaped scroll onto the nautilus. *NOTE: It doesn't have to match the pattern exactly. The pattern is only a general guide for the scrollwork.*

5 Remove scrollwork pattern or fold it back and out of the way. Using single strand of light-colored beading thread and size 15 beading needle, backstitch the scroll with micro- tube beads. When scroll is complete, take needle to back of fabric and out of the way, but do not knot off. Draw a second scroll connected to your first one. Backstitch the second scroll. Continue adding beaded scrolls and spirals to the nautilus design. Feel free to do your own free-form pattern, if you're comfortable with that.

Finish the Wall Hanging

Running stitch completed around three edges of panel.

1 As you've been beading, you've probably noticed the silk raveling at the edges. This is desirable, as we will use that to our advantage to complete this piece. To create a border and also give the silk a point at which to stop raveling, use metallic Fine Braid embroidery thread to make a simple running stitch (see diagram) border. Knot end of thread and start the running stitch at a top corner of the panel. Be sure to place the knot at the front of the panel, as it will be turned under and hidden later. Make stitches approximately ¼" long and place stitches ¼" apart around the sides and bottom of the panel, ½" from the edges.

2 Fold top of panel over ¼" on the front with knot placed at back. Make the same running stitch through both layers across the top to secure and create a casing.

3 Insert hanging hardware, or make a hanger with dowel and cord, if desired.

EMBROIDERY STITCHES

Running Stitch

This is a very simple stitch. Bring needle up at A and take down at B and up at C. Keep going up and down making a straight stitch each time. Vary the lengths of the stitches and the spaces in between for interest.

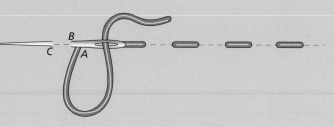

GIFT BAG

I believe it was the color of the chartreuse beads that inspired me to stitch my first peacock feather using size 11/0 beads. I eventually tried size 15/0 and liked the more delicate effect. On the opposite side of the gift bag is a silk ribbon design that's a cinch to blanket stitch and bead-embellish. Whenever you combine velvet and beads, you can't go wrong!

techniques

Covering a design with beads is quite easy and very gratifying. See for yourself as you make the eye of the peacock feather using the beaded backstitch you learned on page 42. You'll also employ the blanket stitch to make a silk ribbon design that lends itself quite willingly to bead embellishment. Couch some fabulous fibers to frame your motifs and put them all together to make a gift bag that will probably outshine what you put inside it.

basic materials

- 2 blue-green 9" x 15" organza
- 2 sets of mixed fiber strands, each 36" long (drawstring)
- Fine-tip black permanent fabric marker
- Iron and ironing board
- Scissors
- Embroidery needle
- Loop turner or similar tool
- Ruler or tape measure

peacock feather materials

- Peacock feather pattern, page 124
- 4½" x 6" fusible interfacing
- 4½" x 6" blue velvet fabric
- 2" x 2" non-fusible interfacing
- ¼ teaspoon blue iris size 10/0 or 11/0 seed beads
- 15 g chartreuse size 15/0 seed beads
- ¼ teaspoon each; teal, blue, purple size 15/0 seed beads
- Crayons or colored pencils: blue, lavender, dark green and yellow green
- Size 13 or 15 beading needle
- Green beading thread
- White or light-colored sewing thread
- Sewing needle
- 1 yd. crinkly yarn (trim)

silk ribbon spiral materials

- Spiral pattern, page 124
- 4" x 6" fusible interfacing
- 4½" x 6½" blue velvet fabric
- 3 yd. 4 mm light blue silk ribbon
- ½ teaspoon pale blue opaque seed beads size 11/0
- Size 10 or 11 beading needle
- Blue beading thread
- Red or contrasting color sewing thread
- 1 yd. twisted blue-and-green chenille yarn (trim)
- Size 8 green metallic Fine Braid embroidery thread
- 100 green iris 5 mm or 6 mm bugle beads
- Embroidery needle
- Sewing needle

bead quantities

Bead quantities are less than one teaspoon/ 5 grams/500 beads for each type, unless otherwise noted. Colors are your choice. Thread quantities are less than a skein or spool, unless otherwise noted. Please read the information in Chapter 1 before starting your project.

Peacock Feather Motif

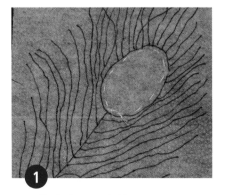

Basting stitches outline eye of feather on front of velvet.

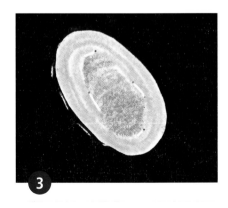

1 Trace feather pattern onto non-adhesive side of fusible interfacing. Fuse to wrong side of velvet.

2 Use sewing thread to baste around eye of feather.

3 Using colored pencils or crayons, trace eye pattern onto non-fusible interfacing. Cut out and baste to front of velvet, inside basted eye outline.

Add Beads

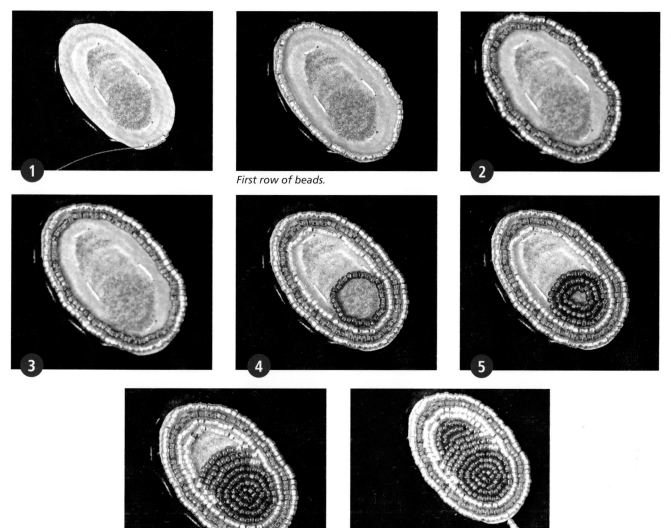

First row of beads.

1 Backstitch (page 42) a row of chartreuse beads around entire perimeter of eye.

2 Backstitch a row of teal beads inside chartreuse row.

3 Notice how the beads in the first two rows do not make smooth ovals (photo 2). To correct this, bring your needle back up through the fabric, next to a bead in the outer row. Insert the needle through the closest chartreuse bead and run needle and thread through all the beads in the outside row. Take it through the first starter bead from this step and a few more beyond it, then go back down through the fabric, pulling the thread to snug the row. When you take out the slack in the thread, all the beads in the row line up evenly. Repeat this process to smooth out the row of teal beads.

4 Backstitch a row of chartreuse beads inside the teal row. Repeat with a row of blue beads inside the chartreuse row, starting at the bottom. Curve the top of the blue row to outline the blue circle within the eye.

5 Backstitch concentric rows of blue beads inside the first row to fill in the blue circle.

6 Backstitch three curved rows of purple beads above the blue circle. Start and end purple rows with a chartreuse bead or two to blend with the feather. Backstitch another row of chartreuse beads inside the third row above the eye with a single blue bead placed at the center top.

7 Backstitch rows of blue beads to fill in the remainder of the eye. Start with the outer rows and work toward the center.

Bead the Rest of the Feather

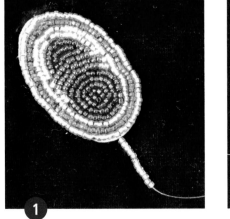

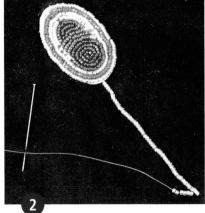

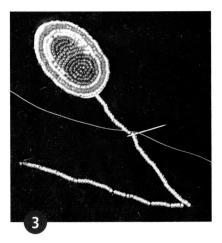

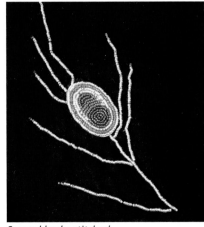

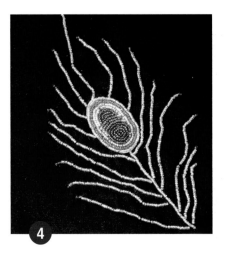

Several barbs stitched.

1 Spine of feather: Refer to pattern on back of velvet and locate the point where the spine descends from the eye. Bring needle up through the velvet at that point and string on six chartreuse beads to start the row of backstitching. Holding the beads against the fabric, turn it over to check the pattern and take the needle down at the spine.

2 Refer to pattern on back. Starting at lower end of spine, backstitch a row of chartreuse beads to make a barb. At tip of barb, add two or three teal beads.

3 Move around the design and stitch barbs to build a framework or foundation for the feather. As you start a new barb, mark its endpoint with a pin so you make stitches in the right direction without looking at the design on the back.

4 Complete a general framework of barbs for the feather. Add more barbs to fill out the feather (see finished photo and pattern). Don't try to follow the pattern exactly, just use it as a general guide.
Note: A few of the barbs cross over each other for a more natural look.

• •

Tip: Place straight pins on front of velvet in a few places along spine to indicate its direction — you won't have to look at the back for each stitch. Check often to be sure you are not getting too far off the mark as you bead.

• •

Ribbon Embroidery Spiral Motif

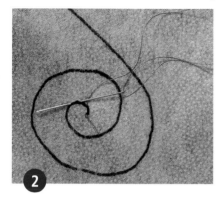

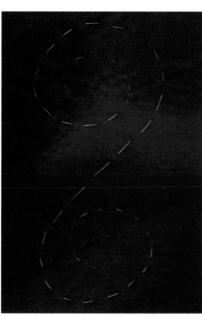

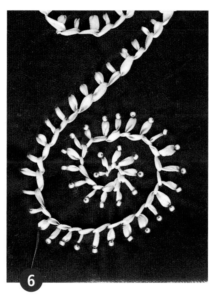

Basted outline of spiral design on front of velvet.

1 Trace spiral pattern onto non-adhesive side of fusible interfacing. Center and fuse to wrong side of velvet.

2 Use sewing thread to baste along lines of design.

3 Using an 18" to 24" length of silk ribbon, start at center of top spiral. Blanket stitch (see diagram) around design.

4 Reload needle with ribbon often and continue blanket stitching entire design. Note how the spokes of the stitches seem to change direction as you curve around the bottom spiral.

5 Remove any basting stitches that show, taking care not to disturb the silk ribbon embroidery.

6 Single stitch a seed bead at the end of each blanket stitched spoke around the entire design.

SILK RIBBON STITCHES
Blanket Stitch

Bring needle up at A, take back down at B and bring back up at C, keeping ribbon under the point of the needle. Pull ribbon slightly to remove slack; allow it to lay on the fabric keeping it as flat as possible.

Starting next stitch, take needle down at D, up at E. Repeat for each stitch. Continue, coming up at D, cross over and take back down at bend, right next to ribbon.

Finish the Gift Bag

1 Fold short side of each organza panel under 3" at top and press. Fold raw edge under ½" and stitch along fold through all layers. Stitch ¾" from top fold to make a casing for the drawstrings.

2 Pin silk ribbon motif to an organza panel.

3 Place end of twisted chenille fiber at bottom of motif. Starting at the center of the motif, use metallic embroidery thread to couch (page 51) the fiber to the panel ¼" from edge of velvet, going through all layers of velvet and organza.

4 Make a couching stitch directly at the first corner. Change direction and proceed to couch up one side, across the top, down the other side and across the bottom, placing a stitch at each corner to change direction. Overlap fiber ends at least 1" at bottom.

5 Using doubled beading thread and beading needle, anchor at back of fabric near base of motif. Bring needle up through bottom front of motif along couched fiber. Pick up a bugle bead and lay across the fiber at slight angle. Single stitch in place. At back of fabric, move needle over about ¼" and come back up to front. Pick up another bugle bead and angle the bead in opposite direction of the first. Stitch in place. Continue around the fiber border with bugle beads.

6 Carefully fringe velvet edges by gently pulling away and removing loose threads. The couching and beadwork create a boundary, preventing the velvet from fraying further.

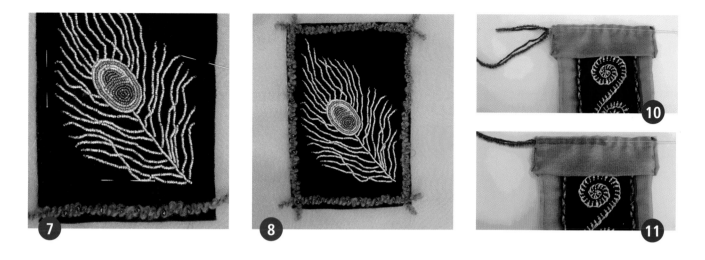

7 Pin peacock feather motif to remaining organza panel. Cut crinkly yarn to extend 1" beyond velvet corners. Using beading needle and doubled strand of beading thread, anchor at back of organza near bottom corner of motif. Bring needle to front and through yarn. Pick up a blue iris seed bead and stitch back through yarn and organza. Repeat around border of velvet, moving needle ⅜" for each stitch. Be sure to catch all layers of fabric and yarn with each stitch. When you reach the opposite corner of the motif, lay down a vertical strip of yarn and continue stitching the side of the frame.

8 When all sides of the frame are stitched in place, neatly trim yarn ends.

9 With right sides together, stitch bag panels around bottom and sides, ending stitching just above and below casing. Turn right-side out and fold top down.

10 Knot one set of fiber drawstrings 2" from each end. Insert loop turner casing and grab knot.

11 Carefully pull one drawstring through casing.

EMBROIDERY STITCHES

Couching

Bring needle up at A, take down at B. Move desired distance at back of fabric and repeat for second stitch.

Vary stitch lengths, angles and distances between stitches for different looks.

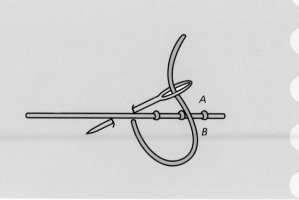

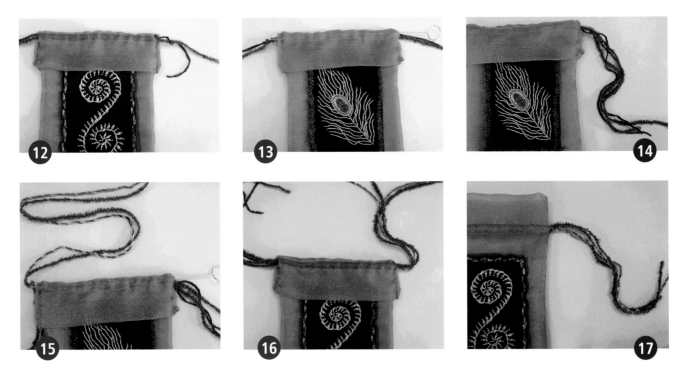

12 Pull ends out through opposite side of casing; remove tool from knot.

13 Turn bag over and feed hook through this casing.

14 Hook into knot at this side of bag and carefully pull fibers through casing so all ends of the drawstring are at one side of the bag.

15 Knot remaining set of fiber drawstrings 2" from each end. Feed hook through casing again and pull second drawstring through.

16 Turn bag over. Feed hook through casing and pull second drawstring through so all the ends of the drawstring are at the opposite side of the bag. You should now have a set of drawstring ends at each side of the bag.

17 Fold top of bag up and pull ends of drawstrings to outside of bag.

SUN PRINTS AND CANISTER

Generally, I don't do a lot of messy, wet, painted or dyed things, but I make an exception when it comes to making "sun prints." This term is a bit misleading, as you don't even need the sun to do this technique. I keep the "mess" contained to a small area so it doesn't overwhelm me. My first experiment got me hooked creating fabric imagery this way.

Fancy pre-beaded trims

materials to make fabric

- 9" x 12" white fabric
- 9" x 12" freezer paper
- 9" x 12" corrugated cardboard or foam core board
- Bulldog clips
- Masking tape
- Heliographic fabric paint: yellow, yellow-green, blue or choice of colors
- Craft sticks
- Paintbrushes: assorted sizes from ¼" to 1" wide
- Water container
- Small paint containers
- Small flat objects, such as leaves, charms, stickers, bits of jewelry, keys, plastic doodads
- Light source (natural sunlight or incandescent)

materials to make canister

- 5" diameter (16" circumference) x 6" tall canister with lid
- 5⅜" x 17" fusible interfacing (or size adjusted to fit your canister)
- 5" square fusible interfacing
- 6" x 11" heliographic image fabric
- 6" x 6" heliographic fabric (lid)
- 6" x 11" complementary novelty fabric
- 6" x 6" plain blue fabric (lid backing)
- 6" pieces pre-beaded fancy trims to cover seams
- 6" piece of 2" or wider ribbon
- ½"- and ¼"-wide super-sticky double-sided tape
- 15" silk-ribbon flower trim
- 17" piece of ¼"-wide flat braid
- 17" piece of ¼"-wide decorative ribbon
- 1 yd. ribbon-type flat trim (lid)
- Assorted seed, bugle and small glass beads
- Chartreuse size 11/0 beads
- Small teardrop beads (lid)
- Size 10 or 11 beading needle
- Beading thread
- Assorted perle cottons
- Assorted Fine Braid metallic embroidery thread
- Embroidery needle
- Fine-tip black permanent fabric marker
- Air-erasable fabric marker
- Fabric stamp with approximate 4" design
- Metallic green fabric paint
- 4½" circle quilt batting
- Removable adhesive dot label
- 24" fuzzy yarn (trim for lid)
- 5" circle of super-sticky double-sided adhesive
- Applicator sponge
- Paint palette
- Heavy-duty sewing thread
- Long sewing needle
- Small flat button
- Large pearl or bead (lid)
- Scissors
- Paper and pencil
- Quick-drying clear glue
- Iron and ironing board
- Small nail and hammer
- Ruler or tape measure
- Optional: sewing machine

techniques

You can purchase lovely, elegant beaded trims. They quickly cover seams while adding beauty and texture — a great alternative to embroidered seams. Go ahead, take the credit when your admirers ooh and aah (after all, you *could* do it!). Rubber stamping with fabric paint is yet another way to create your own imagery on fabric and you'll get a taste of that here. Use techniques learned from other projects and make a stunning container from a humble dollar-store tin.

bead quantities

Bead quantities are less than one teaspoon/5 grams/500 beads for each type, unless otherwise noted. Colors are your choice. Thread quantities are less than a skein or spool, unless otherwise noted. Please read the information in Chapter 1 before starting your project.

Heliographic painting

1 Prepare a surface for painting. Tape freezer paper (shiny side down) to cardboard using masking tape at corners.

2 Clip white fabric to prepared surface at each corner.

3 Scoop out a small amount of paint with a craft stick and place into a small container. Dilute with a few drops of water and stir. Test a drop of the mixture on a paper towel; add desired water, a few drops at a time, to get the intensity of color you like, or use undiluted. Prepare two to four colors of paint in this manner. Using a ¾"-wide brush, dip into first color (I used yellow) and randomly add paint to your fabric.

4 Repeat the paint application step with second color (I used yellow-green). Don't think about making a design, just get some color onto the fabric.

5 Move to third color (I used blue) and perhaps a smaller brush. Apply dabs, swirls or any pattern desired. When blue and yellow overlap, another shade of green results. Remember, don't get too caught up in trying to make a specific design — the point is to cover the fabric with paint.

6 While fabric is still wet, lay stickers, leaves and other flat objects on the surface. When the process works well, wherever an object was placed, a muted lighter image of that shape appears on the fabric. You can't predict the results, so try all sorts of things you have on hand. It's important to have as much object-to-surface contact as possible for the heliographic process to work.

7 If stickers start to lift at the edges, as often happens when wet paint meets dry paper, use straight pins to hold the edges down.

8 Set the panel aside to dry completely. Speed the process by setting it outside on a dry sunny day. It also will work if you leave it in the ambient daylight or incandescent light of your work area.

9 When the fabric is dry to the touch, carefully remove the stickers and objects to reveal the heliographic images.

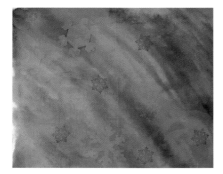

This sheet of fabric was prepared with shades of blue and purple paint and snowflake-shaped objects. After it was dry, and the heliographic images revealed, additional images were added using a snowflake stamp and purple fabric ink.

I prepared this fabric panel for the sides of the canister. The white spirals were punched from plain white paper. The heart shape is a large flat plastic "gem" and the shiny leaf and snowflake are sequins.

This is the final result of the previous photo. Some objects heliograph better than others, but you can't really count on anything behaving the same way from one time to the next. Be prepared to be surprised each time you do this technique!

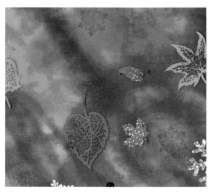

Additional paint (same colors) and objects were added in this example. The finished result was used for the lid of the canister.

Here is an example of a "success" and a not-so-great result. I started with turquoise satin fabric (the way it came from the factory) and used teal heliographic paint. The spider web and spider came from the same sticker sheet. You can see the pinholes where I anchored the stickers down. I was quite pleased with the web, but not with the spider. See how I got around that little challenge in the Sampler Square, page 109. The point is, even if it doesn't turn out as you hoped, you can always find a way to use your experiments somewhere in your crazy quilt projects.

Wrap the Canister

Diagram A
Measure height for fabric panel from bottom of lid to bottom of canister.

1 Measure around your canister and add 1" to each end. Cut fusible interfacing to that measurement and height from bottom of lid to bottom of canister (Diagram A). Mark overlap areas on ends of interfacing.

2 Arrange alternating novelty and heliographic fabrics. Cut at angles onto adhesive side of interfacing between overlap marks. Overlap the fabrics at least ½" to ensure no gaps. Press to fuse fabric to interfacing.

3 Arrange fancy trims to cover seams. Stitch in place with invisible sewing stitches using thread color to blend with trims and fabric.

4 Embellish fabric with trim and beads as desired. Sample shown has a row of magenta embroidery thread featherstitched partially across the panel and a row of backstitching, alternating bugle and seed beads. Narrow silk-ribbon-flower trim was added. These are all randomly intertwining embellishments. Additionally, the imagery in the painted fabric was embellished with single-stitched beads wherever they could be included, sometimes following the shapes in the fabric and sometimes meandering. Loops of strung green seed beads at the end of a spiral image dangle freely from the finished canister.

5 Finish right edge of panel by placing 2" (or wider) ribbon over the fabric, angled to match the other seams, and blanket stitch in place. Trim fabric and interfacing beneath ribbon to ¾" wide. Wrap ribbon around the edge, making sure the covered edge will overlap the other end of the fabric at least ½" when placed around the canister.

6 Stitch fancy trim onto folded ribbon.

7 Blanket stitch along folded edge of ribbon.

8 Apply super-sticky tape to back of finished ribbon edge.

9 Apply ½"-wide super-sticky tape to canister bottom and top, below rim of lid. Apply a vertical strip between the horizontal ones. Remeasure height of completed fabric panel and trim, if necessary, so the lid will not hit the fabric once it has been applied to the canister.

10 Lay canister on its side and remove the protective tape liners. Position unfinished fabric edge onto vertical tape strip and match top and bottom edges of fabric to tape on canister. Slowly roll canister and attach fabric at top and bottom edges, keeping fabric smooth and taut. Remove liner from tape on back of finished ribbon edge and firmly apply finished edge over unfinished edge of fabric.

11 Apply ¼"-wide super-sticky tape to bottom and top edges of fabric panel on canister.

12 Remove liner and press ¼" flat braid onto tape at bottom edge. Trim ends to meet and press firmly to tape. Repeat to apply ¼" decorative ribbon around top edge.

Finish the Lid

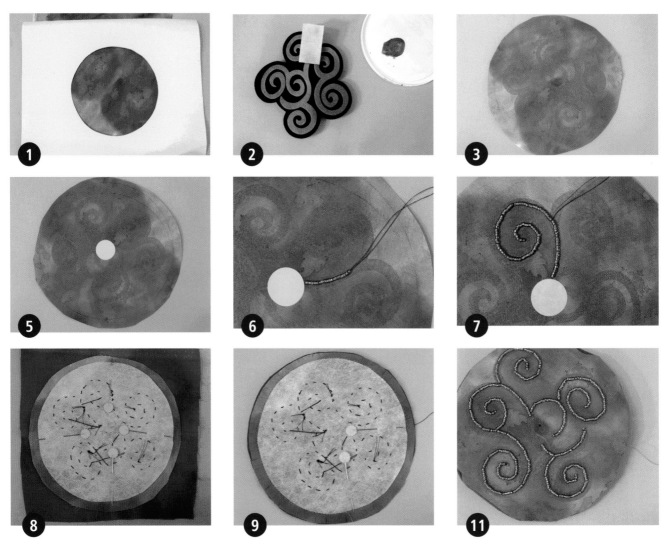

1 Trace around lid on paper and cut out circle template. Place template on heliographic fabric and trace with air-erasable marker.

Note: If you change your mind, as I did, and want to use a different portion of the fabric, that's no problem, the marker will disappear and no one will be the wiser.

2 Place a small amount of green fabric paint on a palette. Dip applicator sponge into paint and tap paint onto fabric stamp. Stamp image onto paper to test. When results are satisfactory, reload stamp with paint and stamp image onto center of lid fabric.

3 Cut out circle of fabric, adding ½" seam allowance.

4 Trace lid onto fusible interfacing and cut out. Fuse to wrong side of lid fabric.

5 Find and mark center of lid fabric with a removable adhesive dot. (This will help you leave an area unbeaded for the knob.)

6 Anchor doubled beading thread to wrong side of fabric. Bring needle up, near dot marker, and backstitch beads onto stamped design.

7 When you finish one spiral element, bring needle up through one or two stitched beads and start next design element; this will help keep the overall design connected. When beadwork is complete, knot off thread on wrong side of fabric and trim tails. Remove marker dot. Re-mark center of lid fabric with fine-tip permanent marker, if necessary.

8 Pin lid fabric to square of plain fabric with right sides together. Stitch, using ½" seam allowance, leaving 2½" opening.

9 Trim plain fabric to match lid and clip curves through both layers.

10 Turn right-side out. Press edges flat. Insert circle of quilt batting between fabric layers.

11 Fold remaining edges of fabric to inside and whipstitch closed.

12 Anchor sewing thread to lid cover at seam. Couch around strand of fuzzy trim and pull tight to anchor it to lid.

13 Slide needle through ½" of lid backing next to seam. Couch around fiber and take a small stitch into fabric. Proceed around lid cover in this manner.

14 Anchor thread and trim fibers, leaving 2" tails.

15 Anchor beading thread to underside of lid cover near edge. Bring needle out through fiber and pick up a teardrop bead. Single stitch bead to edge of lid cover and slide needle ⅜" away from stitch to begin next stitch. Single stitch teardrops around entire lid cover.

16 Mark center of lid. Use small nail with hammer to punch a hole large enough to accommodate a large sewing needle. Apply a small piece of ½" super-sticky tape to rim. Remove paper liner.

17 Affix one end of ribbon-type trim to tape and wrap around rim twice to cover metal. Secure to tape and trim end.

18 Trim 5" circle of super-sticky double-sided adhesive ⅛" smaller than top of lid. Apply to lid and remove paper liner. Carefully apply lid cover to lid.

19 Place small button against hole at underside of lid. Thread sturdy sewing needle with heavy-duty thread, pass through buttonhole in lid and bring up at center of lid cover, leaving a long thread tail at underside of lid. String on large bead or pearl and a smaller stop bead (as small as the needle can pass through) to hold the large bead in place. Pass needle back through large bead hole in lid and button. Tie off thread ends firmly with several knots. Secure with a drop of glue and trim ends of tails.

EYEGLASS POUCH

The beaded chain stitch is a good way to outline motifs with two rows of beads at once. It's the perfect vehicle for making a stylized Celtic knot using two bead colors. If you look closely, you'll see how the strips of colors overlap each other, intertwining the overall design.

Prepare the pattern

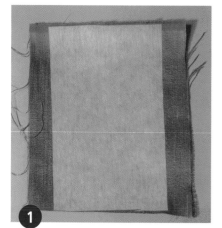

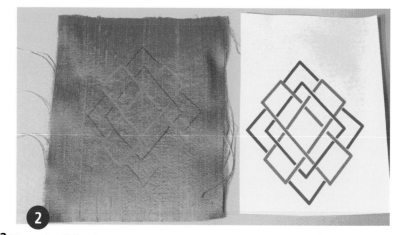

1 Reinforce silk by centering from side to side and fusing interfacing to back. *Note: Your silk will ravel along the edges as you work and you'll end up with a much narrower piece than you started with!*

2 Trace the Celtic knot pattern onto tracing paper using colored pencils. Place and center tracing under silk panel on a light box or other light source. Retrace lines on silk using the blue and green pencils as indicated on the pattern. Note where pattern lines are broken — follow closely while beading (beaded chain stitch, page 69).

materials

- Celtic pattern, page 125
- Assembly diagram, page 68
- 5" x 6" blue silk
- 3½" x 6" fusible interfacing
- 3¾" x 13" fancy fabric (pouch)
- 3¾" x 18" fabric (lining)
- Soft-lead colored pencils: blue, green
- Tracing paper
- 2 to 3 strands blue size 11/0 beads
- 1 teaspoon green iris size 11/0 beads
- Size 10 or 11 beading needle
- Beading thread
- Iron and ironing board
- Light box or other light source for pattern transfer
- Sewing needle and thread or sewing machine with standard foot and zipper foot

techniques

Working out the over-under method for this design was akin to a brain-teaser. You can't just make one whole section of the beaded design and then go to the next…the only way to have each color crossover each other is by doing several stops and starts. Nevertheless, this is a fun and highly rewarding project to make.

bead quantities

Bead quantities are less than one teaspoon/5 grams/500 beads for each type, unless otherwise noted. Colors are your choice. Thread quantities are less than a skein or spool, unless otherwise noted. Please read the information in Chapter 1 before starting your project.

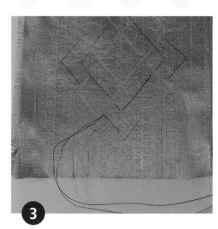

3 Anchor doubled beading thread at back of silk at starting point (A) of Section 1 (outside edge of blue line; see diagram page 64).

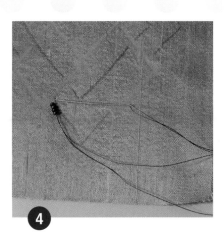

4 Pick up four blue beads; slide up to fabric. Insert needle into fabric at point B, inside of blue line and parallel to A. Take needle to back of fabric and arrange beads to form a loop with two sets of beads side by side covering the blue pattern line.

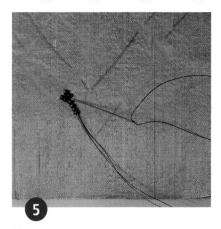

5 Bring thread back up between the legs of beads in first stitch. Pick up four beads; slide next to first two beads. Take needle back through fabric, inside of bead loop from first stitch.

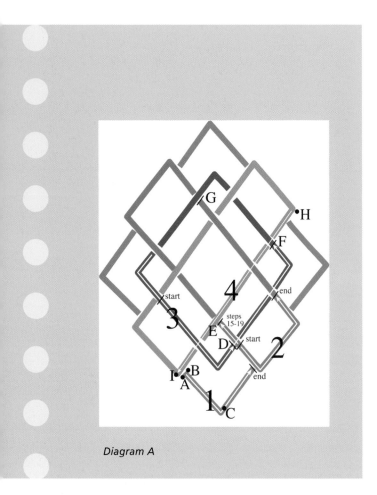

Diagram A

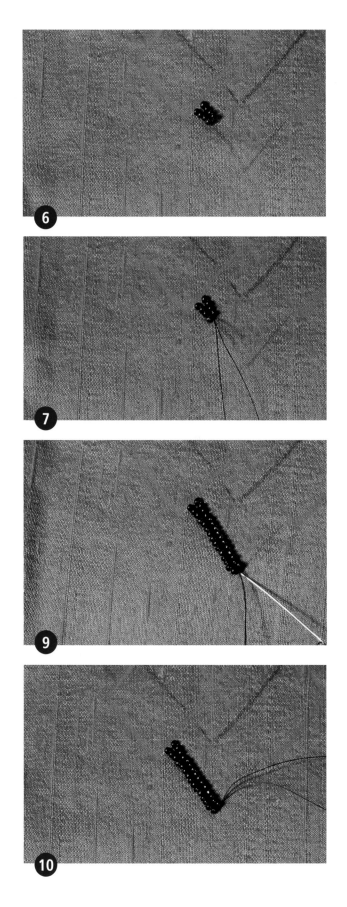

6 Pull thread all the way to back and arrange the last four beads to form a loop with two beads per leg. Line up with legs from first stitch.

7 Bring thread back up between the legs of beads in last stitch.

8 Pick up four more beads and make a new bead loop.

9 Continue stitching beads in along the pattern line with each stitch, beginning and ending inside the previous stitch, until you reach the bend in Section 1. Bring needle up through last stitch, but instead of picking up more beads, stitch across the center of the loop and back into fabric, anchoring the loop end.

10 Bring needle back up at C (see Diagram A) and start the new row of Section 1.

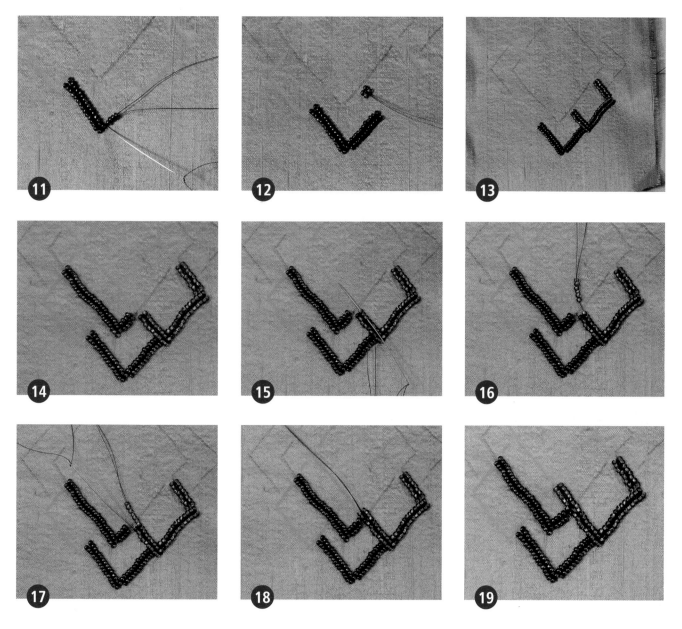

11 Pick up four beads and take needle down at outside of pattern line. Continue chain stitching to end of Section 1.

12 Anchor thread at back of silk to start Section 2. Pick up four green beads and make the first stitch.

13 Stitch Section 2, anchoring rows and changing direction twice.

14 Switch back to blue beads and work part of Section 3, stopping at point D. Anchor the last loop.

15 Bring needle up through Section 2 and slide through three beads at "north" end, adding to Section 2.

16 Pick up four beads.

17 Make stitch, taking thread to back at other side of pattern line so the new beads line up with earlier beads.

18 Bring thread out inside of last stitch and continue with next stitch.

19 Work the short distance to point E, then anchor last loop.

Bridge the Beaded Stitches

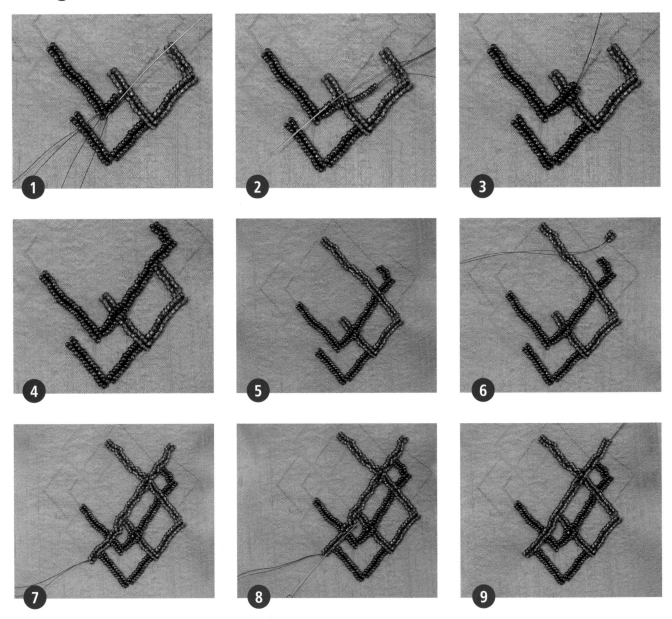

1 Bring needle up and through three of the beads in the portion of blue Section 3 at D.

2 Pick up 12 to 14 blue beads. Take needle back through the blue bead opposite the one you exited from and down to back of fabric.

3 Bring needle up inside of loop, which should lay across or "bridge" the green beads.

4 Continue beading Section 3 using four or six beads for each stitch and anchoring the row to change direction. End Section 3 at point F.

5 Bring needle out through three beads of Section 2 (green) and continue Section 2 with a bridge over the blue beads in Section 3. Bead Section 2 to point G and anchor end.

6 Begin Section 4 at point H using green beads.

7 Stitch Section 4 to point I, bridging green Section 2 as shown, and anchor end. Note how crooked this row is.

8 Straighten the last row of beads stitched by taking needle back through beads on one side of row.

9 Bring needle out at end of row. Pull thread slightly to take up slack and the row will straighten.

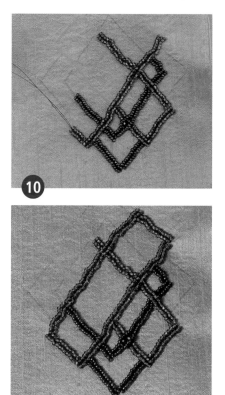

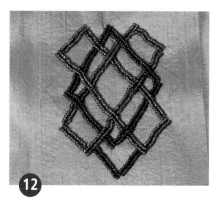

Section 4 completed.

10 Return needle through other side of row, back to point I. Anchor thread by taking a stitch through fabric. Change direction and continue beading Section 4 around all sides, bridging Section 2 once more. Use technique in Step 9 to straighten crooked rows as needed.

11 Finish beading blue Section 3, bridging Section 4 three times as shown.

12 Finish beading green Section 2 and blue Section 1, bridging other sections as shown. Straighten crooked rows as needed.

Assemble Pouch

1 Sew beaded silk flap to pouch fabric, right sides together, using ¼" or ⅜" seam allowance. Press seam toward pouch and topstitch ¼" from seam on pouch.

2 Pin pouch and flap to lining with right sides together.

Assembly Diagram

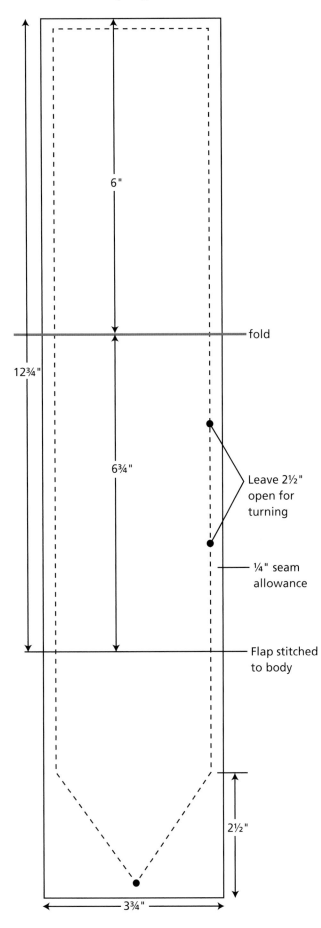

6"

12¾"

6¾"

fold

Leave 2½"
open for
turning

¼" seam
allowance

Flap stitched
to body

2½"

3¾"

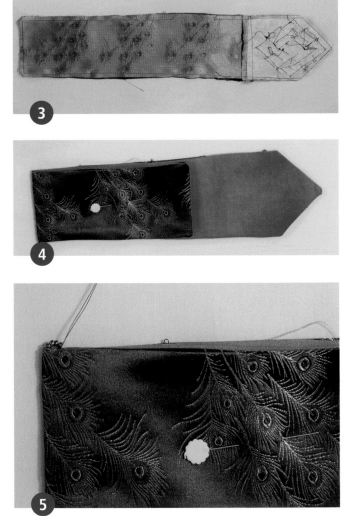

3 Refer to Assembly Diagram and mark center point on flap,
¼" from beadwork. Machine stitch lining to pouch and flap
using zipper foot, or by hand using ¼" seam allowance. Leave
2½" open at one side of pouch for turning. Trim corners and
point of flap.

4 Turn right-side out and press seams flat. Fold pouch body
as shown in Assembly Diagram and pin.

5 Add beaded edging (page 69) to close pouch sides and
finish edge in one step. Begin by anchoring doubled beading
thread at bottom corner inside fold. Bring needle out to front
of corner and pick up four green iris beads. Make a short
stitch, taking needle from back to front, catching both layers
of pouch fabric (lining too, if desired). The stitch should be
long enough for the beads to lie flat (or almost flat) and hold
the front and back panels of the pouch together.

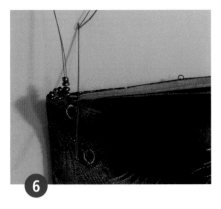

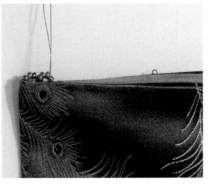

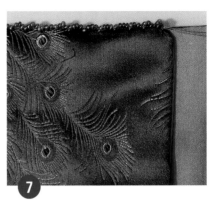

Second beaded edge stitch completed. Note that the thread is emerging from the front of the pouch.

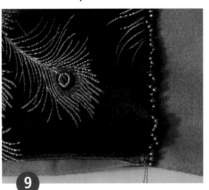

Side view of beaded edging.

6 Pick up four more beads. Your thread should be emerging from the front layer of the pouch at this point. Take next stitch, starting through back of pouch and coming out through front as shown.

7 Continue along edge of pouch in this manner. When you reach the top edge, anchor thread securely at corner and come through the top layer only of the pouch.

8 Bead across top edge of pouch, taking stitches through pouch front and front lining only.

9 Anchor thread, once again, at opposite corner.

10 Bead down the second side of pouch, through all fabric layers, joining front to back with beaded edging.

BEAD STITCHES

Beaded Chain Stitch

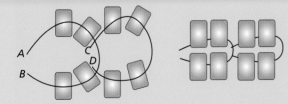

Bring needle up at A, pick up four beads and go back down at B, close to A. Bring needle up at C, inside bead loop. Pick up four beads and go back at D, close to C. Repeat. When slack is removed from thread, the beads will lie close together and look like two continuous rows of beads.

Beaded Edging

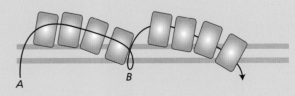

Bring needle up at A through two layers of fabric. Take down at B, catching only one layer of fabric. Go back up through both layers close to B, pick up four beads and repeat.

STRAWBERRY POCKET PURSE

This purse started out with a wild goose chase. I spent a few hours driving to a Crazy Quilters' Show only to arrive at a small conventional quilt show sponsored by a quilting guild that used crazy in their name. As long as I was there, I walked the show and happened upon a vendor with the most luscious

hand-dyed velvets. The red called to me the loudest. I could only afford ¼ yard and had no idea what I'd use it for. Months later, the idea for plump, juicy strawberry appliqués popped into my head. Conveniently, I had just the fabric in my stash to act on the impulse.

Prep Fabric Pieces

1 Cut lining and flap of pocketbook as directed on page 72.   **2** Fuse interfacing to wrong side of flap.

Dimensional Strawberry Appliqués

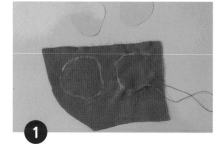
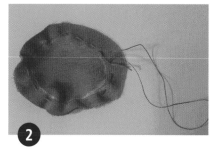
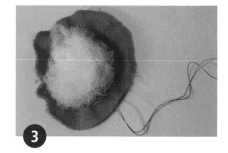

1 Using graphite paper, transfer berry patterns to card stock and cut out shapes. Draw around berry templates on wrong side of red velvet using quilting pencil or chalk. With sewing needle and doubled red thread knotted at end, run a basting stitch around the pattern lines of one berry. Leave needle threaded and attached so you can pull up gathers in a later step.

2 Carefully cut berry shape from velvet, adding ¼" to ⅜" seam allowance, taking care not to cut thread from Step 1.

3 Place a small amount (just a pinch) of fiberfill in center of berry and begin to pull up gathering thread.

materials

- Pattern, page 123
- Cutting diagram, page 72
- 8½" x 11" red silk fabric (purse body)
- 8½" x 6" black-and-gold polka dot velvet fabric (flap)
- 8½" x 16¼" red satin fabric (lining)
- 4" x 6" red velvet fabric
- 4¼" x 7½" fusible interfacing
- Size 11/0 seed beads: clear yellow or gold, red, black and metallic gold
- 1 yd. 7 mm variegated green silk embroidery ribbon
- Size 5 green perle cotton
- Size 8 black perle cotton
- Red sewing thread
- Graphite transfer paper
- 4" x 6" paper card stock
- Small amount of fiberfill
- White quilting pencil or chalk
- Sewing needle
- Size 10 or 11 beading needle
- Beading thread
- Embroidery needle
- Iron and ironing board
- Scissors
- Ruler or tape measure
- Optional: sewing machine

techniques

Dimensional appliqués add interest and drama to a quilted piece, and the strawberries are quick to make. If you don't want to use red velvet or red silk, another special fabric would work as well. The little seed beads dimple the fabric just as seeds dimple the surface of a real strawberry. The black velvet used for the backdrop was another accidental discovery — the gold dots are paint, and although the fabric came that way, it would be easy enough to transform plain black velvet with dimensional fabric paint to look the same.

bead quantities

Bead quantities are less than one teaspoon/5 grams/500 beads for each type, unless otherwise noted. Colors are your choice. Thread quantities are less than a skein or spool, unless otherwise noted. Please read the information in Chapter 1 before starting your project.

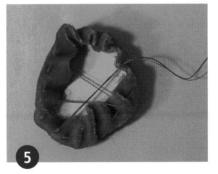

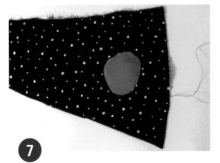

4 Insert berry template into gathered fabric and pull gathering stitches to surround template; do not pull so tightly that the template buckles or bends.

5 Stitch across berry to hold gathered edges against template. Anchor thread but leave on needle.

6 Place berry on flap as shown, keeping well clear of seam allowance. Using red thread still attached, make a small stitch to anchor the berry to the flap.

7 Whipstitch (page 10) around berry, and using small stitches, attach to flap.

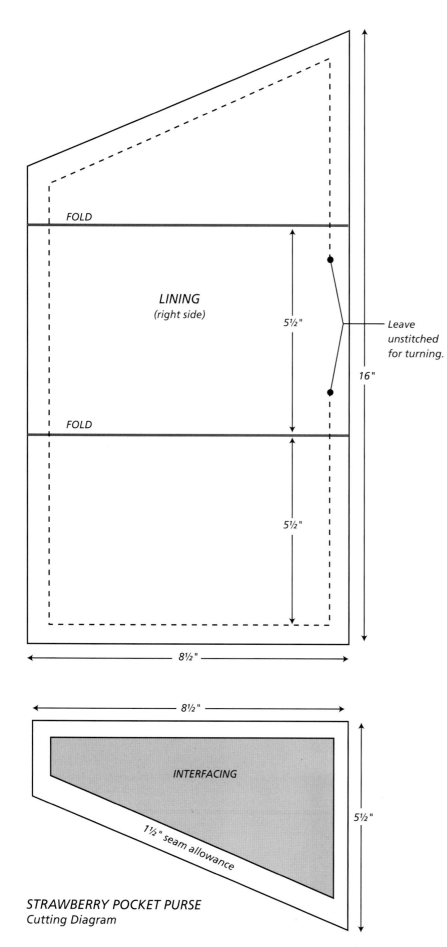

FOLD

LINING
(right side)

5½"

16"

Leave
unstitched
for turning.

FOLD

5½"

8½"

8½"

INTERFACING

1½" seam allowance

5½"

STRAWBERRY POCKET PURSE
Cutting Diagram

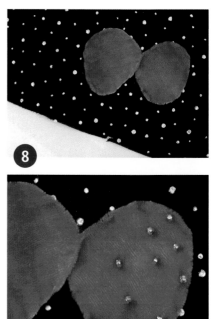

8

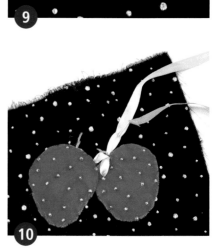

9

10

8 Prepare second berry and stitch to flap, overlapping first berry slightly as shown.

9 Use single or doubled beading thread and needle to single stitch clear yellow or gold seed beads randomly over berries. With each stitch, pull thread slightly to create a small dimple on the berry's surface.

10 Use green perle cotton to make a split stitch (page 73) stem on each berry. Using embroidery needle and silk ribbon, add bracts to berry tops using ribbon stitch (page 73).

EMBROIDERY STITCH

Split Stitch

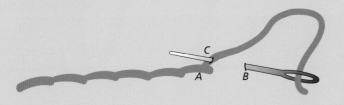

Use size 5 or larger embroidery thread for best results. Bring needle up at A, down at B and back up at A, splitting the thread with each stitch.

SILK RIBBON EMBROIDERY

Ribbon Stitch

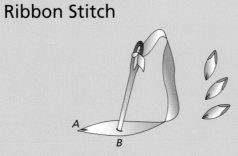

Bring needle up at A, holding ribbon flat against fabric. Take needle down at B, pulling gently to make the sides of ribbon curl slightly inward. Do not put too much tension on the ribbon or the curls will disappear.

Assemble the Purse

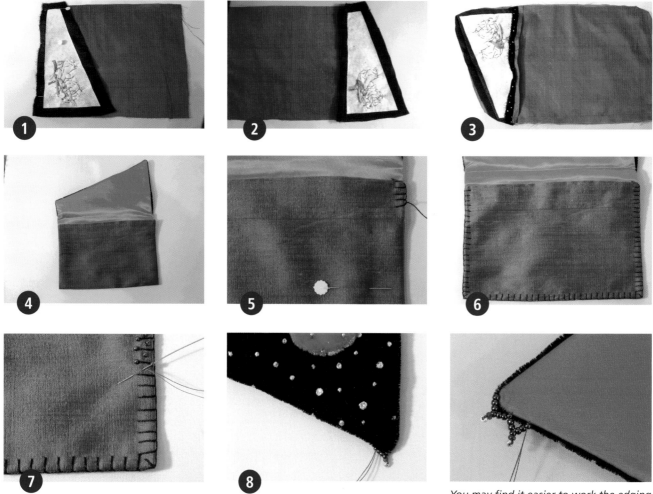

You may find it easier to work the edging from the backside of the flap, stitching into the flap lining.

1 With right sides together, pin flap to top edge of pocket-book body.

2 Stitch flap to body using ½" seam allowance.

3 Stitch flap and body to lining, right sides together, leaving opening for turning as marked on diagram (page 72). Clip corners.

4 Turn right-side out and press seams. Fold body of purse up to flap seam as shown.

5 Join sides of pocketbook using black perle cotton and blanket stitches (page 16). Hide knot inside and start at top corner. Bring needle out through side seam of body. Make a small straight stitch to start. Blanket stitch through all layers of body around sides and bottom.

6 At corners, make a shorter stitch and anchor it before changing direction. Anchor last stitch at opposite top corner and hide thread tails inside of purse.

7 Stitch a single black seed bead between and at end of each blanket stitch. Hide knot inside of purse to begin. Bring needle to front of fabric and stitch beads only to the front and front lining of the purse.

8 Add beaded edging to flap: Anchor beading thread in seam of flap edge. Pick up four black seed beads, one red seed and one gold metallic seed. *Go back through red and one black bead and pick up three black beads. Make stitch in edge of flap. Pick up three black beads, one red bead and one gold bead. Repeat from * to complete stitching along bottom edge of flap.

9 Knot off beading thread and hide in seam of flap edge.

DOORKNOB POUCH WITH GRAPES

Grape motifs have long been a favorite of mine, so I've developed a few ways to include them in my crazy quilting. This is perhaps the easiest way, using hot-fix Austrian crystals to enhance an inkjet-on-fabric design. Tuck notes or small whatnots into the pouch and hang it on a doorknob or chest of drawers.

materials

- Grapes image, page 128
- 25 heliotrope 3 mm hot-fix rhinestones
- 4" x 8" fabric (backing)
- 2¾" x 6½" fusible interfacing
- 7" x 8" fabric (lining)
- 26" of 1½"-wide ribbon, cut 2 pieces 8½" and 2 pieces 4½"
- 18" thick yarn or fiber (framing)
- 1 teaspoon turquoise size 11/0 matte finish seed beads
- 28 grams assorted focal beads (handle and fringe)
- 1 teaspoon assorted seed beads (handle and fringe)
- Size 8 magenta metallic Fine Braid embroidery thread
- Inkjet printable fabric
- Computer with scanner and inkjet printer
- Electric rhinestone applicator
- Embroidery needle
- Sewing needle and thread
- Size 10 or 11 beading needle
- Beading thread
- Scissors
- Iron and ironing board
- Ruler or tape measure
- Optional: sewing machine

techniques

Couch a frame using beads to stitch and hold down fibers. Embellish your pouch with a fringing technique using a variety of beads. As always, any of the techniques, and the patch itself, could be incorporated into other crazy quilt projects.

bead quantities

Bead quantities are less than one teaspoon/5 grams/500 beads for each type, unless otherwise noted. Colors are your choice. Thread quantities are less than a skein or spool, unless otherwise noted. Please read the information in Chapter 1 before starting your project.

Print Fabric and Apply Rhinestones

1 Using your computer, scan the grapevine image on page 128. Place on a document page, test on paper, then print onto inkjet fabric.

2 Use electric rhinestone applicator and attach rhinestones to image on top of grapes. Follow instructions included with appliance.

Frame the Image

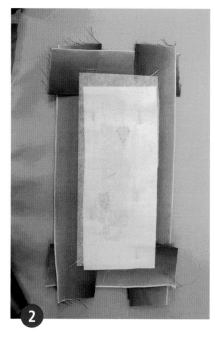

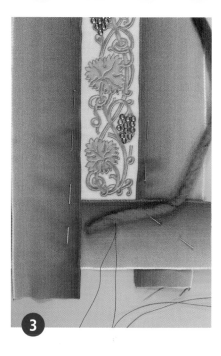

1 Pin ribbons around image, overlapping ends log cabin style. The inside edges of the ribbon should cover the white margins of the fabric, but not grapevines in image.

2 Turn image over and fuse interfacing to center back. This reinforces and helps connect ribbon edging to fabric.

3 Anchor doubled beading thread at bottom center to back of fabric. Lay thick yarn against ribbon edge, next to image. Take a small stitch and attach it to the layers of fabric and ribbon.

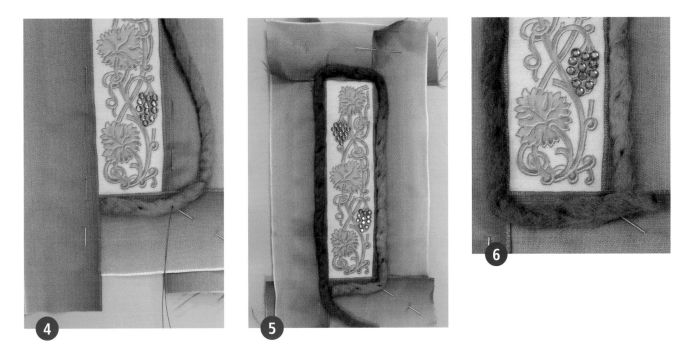

4 Take a second small stitch through yarn and fabric at corner of frame.

5 Continue stitching around frame, placing a stitch at each corner so you easily can take the yarn in a different direction.

6 Overlap ends of yarn at bottom, and stitch through all layers. Trim end of top yarn so it extends beyond the corner slightly. Knot thread at back of fabric.

Couch the Yarn

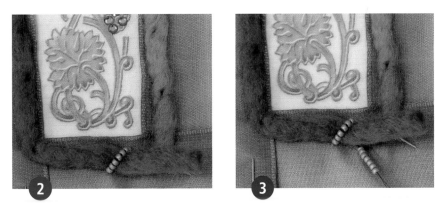

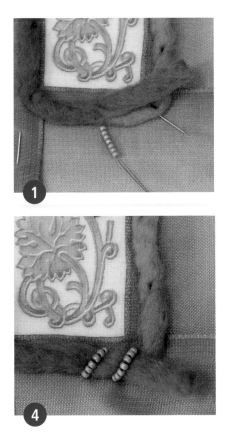

1 Using doubled beading thread, bring beading needle out through front of fabric just below the overlapped yarn ends. Pick up seven beads (more or less, depending on thickness of yarn) and slide towards fabric.

2 Take needle back through fabric, just above yarn, and slightly to right. Make angled stitch as shown.

3 Bring needle back up through fabric below yarn, parallel to last entry point. Pick up seven beads (or same number as in Step 1).

4 Move needle slightly to the right and go back down above yarn and into fabric. Space the stitches, landing one in the corner of the yarn as shown. It may be your third or fourth stitch, depending on your stitch length and where you started.

5 Bring needle up at outside edge of corner, pick up beads, and go back down at same point as in Step 4. This will pivot the stitching around the corner.

6 Proceed to couch with beads, making angled stitches around the yarn frame. Each time you reach a corner, make a pivot stitch as in Step 5.

7 Carefully trim end of top yarn close to a couching stitch.

8 Using embroidery needle and metallic embroidery thread, stitch ribbon edges to outside corners using small running stitches (page 44).

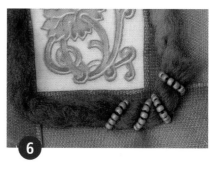

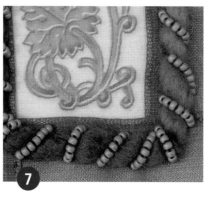
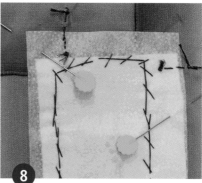

Assemble the Pouch

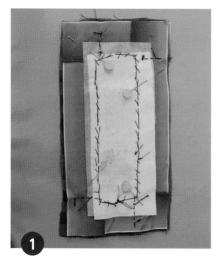
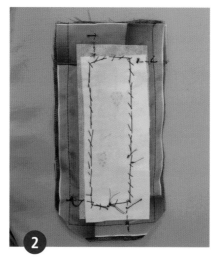

1 With right sides together, pin pouch front to backing fabric.

2 Stitch pouch to back at sides and bottom using ½" seam allowance. Clip bottom corners. Turn right-side out.

3 Fold lining fabric in half lengthwise, right sides together. Stitch side and bottom using ½" seam allowance and leaving a 3" opening along side seam for turning. Clip corner.

4 Place pouch into lining, right sides together, and pin.

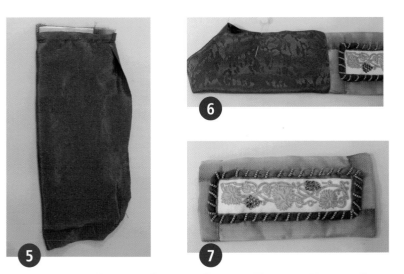

5 Stitch around top, joining lining to pouch, using ½" seam allowance.

6 Turn right-side out and pin lining at opening. Whipstitch (page 10) closed.

7 Insert lining into pouch.

Bead the Hanger and Fringe the Bottom

1 Anchor doubled beading thread at top corner of pouch. String on assorted focal beads to 9" or desired length. Anchor at opposite side of pouch. Restring through all beads to reinforce. Anchor at original corner and trim thread tails.

2 Anchor doubled beading thread at bottom center of pouch seam. String on seed and focal beads to 3" or desired length, ending with a small seed (stop bead). Go back through all beads except stop bead and make stitch into pouch bottom.

3 Move thread to right, one or two seed bead widths, and bring out of fabric. String on assorted beads making a shorter length than previous strand. Use a seed bead at end as a stop bead.

4 Continue working to the right, making progressively shorter strands. Anchor last strand at outer corner. Re-anchor thread to just left of center strand and repeat the beading sequence in reverse to create a symmetrical fringe.

GRAPES ALL AROUND NECKLACE

Here's a different technique you can use to make grapes. They are easy to replicate with beads and thread. The shapes are simple spheres and the overall shape of a grape cluster is tapered at the bottom. Leaves and stems easily complete the realistic look of this versatile fruit.

Prepare the Ribbon

1 Center and fuse two layers of interfacing to back of ribbon for reinforcement (one layer on top of the other).

2 Fold ribbon in half crosswise and press at fold.

3 Using doubled beading or sewing thread and appropriate needle, tack a velvet or silk leaf to one layer of the ribbon.
Note: The top of the panel is the fold. Open up ribbon to avoid catching both layers while stitching.

materials

- Grape pattern template, page 123
- 7½" of 2"-wide ribbon
- 2 pieces 6½" x 1¾" fusible interfacing
- 2½" bead fringe (pre-stitched to ribbon or twill tape)
- 1 each of 2 styles velvet or silk floral leaves
  Note: Vintage velvet leaves are available through specialty fabric shops.
  If you can't find them, remove a leaf from a stem of silk flowers!
- 4 yd. variegated purple chenille yarn
- Large-eye embroidery needle
  Note: A heavy needle will work best for this project. The eye is larger
  to more readily accommodate the yarn and the shaft will make a
  larger hole in the fabric, making it easier to coax the chenille through.
  Remember, chenille is intended for knitting and we are using it here for
  sewing.
- 2 teaspoon purple size 8/0 seed beads
- 20 clear purple size 5/0 or 6/0 rocaille beads
- 1 yd. lightweight green yarn or size 3 embroidery thread
- 1 yd. pale green ¼"-wide sheer organza ribbon (neck strap)
- Tracing paper
- Pencil
- 2" square card stock
- Graphite transfer paper
- Size 10 or 11 beading needle
- Beading thread
- Scissors
- Iron and ironing board
- Ruler or tape measure
- Optional: Sewing thread and needle

techniques

Learn two different techniques to make stunning grape clusters, one using luscious beads and the other using scrumptious chenille fibers. For variations, try other colors — after all, in nature grapes come in many shades of green, red, blue and purple.

bead quantities

Bead quantities are less than one teaspoon/5 grams/500 beads for each type, unless otherwise noted. Colors are your choice. Thread quantities are less than a skein or spool, unless otherwise noted. Please read the information in Chapter 1 before starting your project.

Make the Template

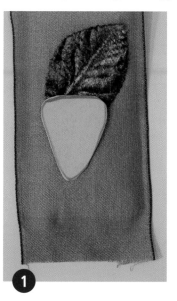

1 Trace template pattern onto tracing paper. Transfer to card stock using graphite paper and cut out. Place template onto ribbon. Cover lower third or quarter of leaf as shown.

2 Trace template on ribbon using air-erasable marker.

Chenille French Knot Grapes

Using Chenille Yarn

Purple chenille yarn.

Tip: When using chenille yarn, you can usually only make two or three stitches before the needle and passage through fabric take their toll and wear out the yarn. (After all, yarn is made to be knitted or crocheted, not make multiple passes through fabric as we are doing.) Therefore, load the needle often using a short length of yarn each time. You can save and couch unused tails to embellish other projects. If you are having trouble getting the chenille yarn through the fabric, try using an awl, skewer or similar tool to make pilot holes for your stitches.

EMBROIDERY STITCHES

French Knot

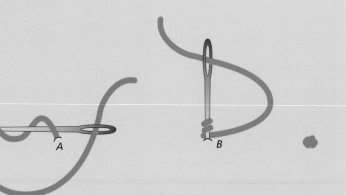

Bring needle up at A. Wrap thread around needle one or more times, pull snug and go back down at B, right next to or in same hole as A.

Note: If thread is wrapped in wrong direction, the stitch will disappear!

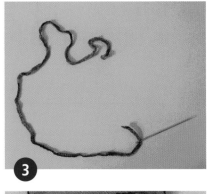

3

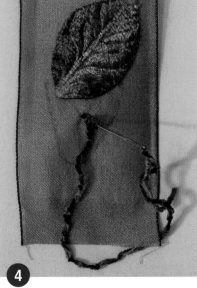

4

5

3 Thread large-eye embroidery needle with a 12" strand of chenille yarn, keeping a very short tail at the eye. Knot opposite end of yarn.

4 Bring needle up near the center of the grape cluster.

5 Make a single French knot (see diagram).

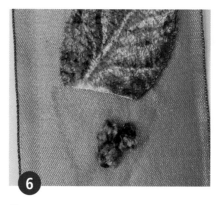

6 Make two more French knots adjacent to first one. Trim away lower edge of leaf at top of cluster as shown.

7 Cover the template area with French knots. Make some of the knots through lower edge of leaf.

8 Using beading thread and needle, randomly single stitch a few size 5/0 or 6/0 rocailles around the cluster.

Beaded Grapes

1 Open up ribbon so the fold is at top of opposite panel. Tack leaf in place using doubled beading thread. Position template and trace lower portion of grape cluster onto ribbon using an air-erasable marker.

2 Single stitch (page 17) size 8/0 beads to fill in around leaf, inside cluster outline.

3 Place template onto beading and leaf to locate top corners of cluster. Mark.

4 Stitch a single bead at each marked upper corner of cluster, directly onto leaf.

5 Single stitch beads to connect one corner to the bottom portion of the cluster.

6 Single stitch beads to the other top corner to connect bottom of cluster.

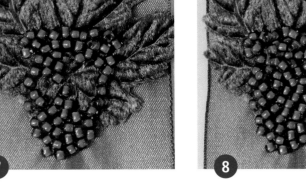

7 Begin to fill in the remainder of cluster with beads.

8 Add a second layer of single-stitched beads to make the cluster dimensional. Start at the top and work down, making the second layer smaller than bottom layer.

9 Using embroidery needle and lightweight green yarn or size 3 green embroidery thread, knot end, and bring up through back of fabric at top of grape cluster. Loosely twist yarn to make a stem. Take end of thread back through fabric and anchor.

10 Using sewing thread, arrange yarn stem and tack to leaf. Fold ribbon raw edges ¼" to inside and pin.

Assemble the Necklace

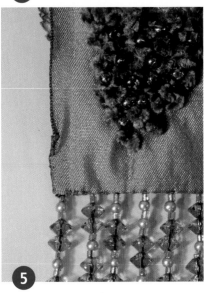

1 Measure bead fringe along bottom edge of necklace. Remove beads from each end of fringe tape, and turn ends under to match width of necklace (or slightly shorter). Tack ends in place.

2 Pin fringe at one end to wrong side of necklace.

3 Cover fringe tape with top layer of necklace. Anchor sewing thread to inside edge of necklace just above fringe tape. Using tiny whipstitches (page 10), sew front and back of necklace along the side, encasing fringe tape as you sew.

4 Continue whipstitching along bottom edge of necklace, taking stitches through front and back of ribbon between bead fringes.

5 Stitch opposite side of necklace to edge of fringe tape.

6 Thread sheer organza ribbon through layers of necklace. Adjust to desired length and knot ends. Stitch ribbon neck strap at top corner edges of necklace.

FOUR STAMPED PATCHES

Now that you have an idea of the projects you can make with your motifs, let's concentrate on a few more techniques. Keep in mind that all of the techniques you're learning can be combined with each other to make a fabulous crazy quilt or a special one-of-a-kind fashion or home décor accessory.

materials for each patch

- 5½" square of fabric
- 4½" square of fusible interfacing
- Iron and ironing board
- Size 10 or smaller beading needle
- Beading thread
- Scissors
- Applicators for applying paint to stamp

materials for filigree heart

- 3" x 3½" filigree heart stamp
- Copper metallic fabric paint
- Metallic cord
- Gold metallic size 11/0 beads

materials for multicolored leaf

- 3" x 3" leaf stamp
- Teal and purple metallic fabric paint
- Clear size 11/0 beads

materials for double heart

- 3" x 3½" heart-in-heart stamp
- 1 teaspoon bronze or gold metallic fabric paint
- Dark blue size 11/0 beads
- Metallic copper size 11/0 beads
- Optional: Small paintbrush

materials for sun

- 4" sun stamp
- 1 teaspoon copper metallic fabric paint
- Shiny orange size 11/0 orange beads
- 2 teaspoons fuchsia size 11/0 matte beads
- 1 orange size 5/0 rocaille

bead quantities

Bead quantities are less than one teaspoon/5 grams/500 beads for each type, unless otherwise noted. Colors are your choice. Thread quantities are less than a skein or spool, unless otherwise noted. Please read the information in Chapter 1 before starting your project.

techniques

The quickest way to get a basic motif image onto your fabric is to use stamps with fabric paint or fabric ink. From large foam décor stamps to intricate rubber stamps, they all can be used. A variety of beading techniques are readily available to embellish them and make each one uniquely yours.

Stamps used to create four different patches.

Stamping on fabric is as simple as applying paint to your stamp and pressing the stamp to your fabric. For a refresher on how to do this, see page 60, Step 2.
Stamp image on fabric and allow to dry completely. Heat set with iron. Reinforce patch by fusing interfacing to back.

Metallic cord.

Filigree Heart

 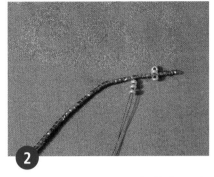 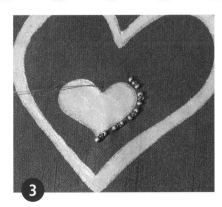

1 Fuse interfacing to fabric. Stamp image at angle as shown.

2 Anchor beading thread at back of fabric near tip of heart image. Bring up and stitch tightly over end of metallic cord once or twice, anchoring it to fabric. At back of fabric, move needle a short distance from cord end and bring up through fabric near edge of image. Pick up three gold beads and slide towards fabric. Take stitch across cord, couching (page 24) it to fabric. Bring needle back up a short distance from first

stitch. Pick up three beads and make second couching stitch across cord.

3 Work stitching around heart. As you reach the top, begin to plan for landing a stitch at the center of the heart and space stitches accordingly. At end, make a stitch at the heart's tip, then take a tight stitch across the end of the cording. Trim cording close to this last stitch. Add a final beaded stitch to cover the cord ends.

Multicolored Leaf

1 Fuse interfacing to fabric. Load stamp with both color paints. Use different applicators to quickly dab each color onto stamp, allowing colors to overlap a little. Press stamp to fabric to transfer image.

2 Randomly single stitch (page 17) clear beads over stamp to resemble dewdrops.

Double Heart

 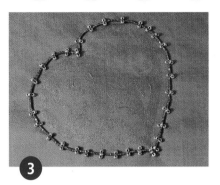

1 Fuse interfacing to fabric. Stamp image on fabric. In this case, the image transferred lighter than desired.

2 Use a paintbrush and paint to touch up and enhance the stamped image. Let dry.

3 Frame the inner heart with three-bead lazy stitches (page 19). Start at tip of heart and bring needle to front of fabric. Pick up beads in this order; one copper, one blue and one copper. Take needle down next to last bead, so beads lie flat against fabric. Move needle, leaving a small gap, then repeat the stitch.

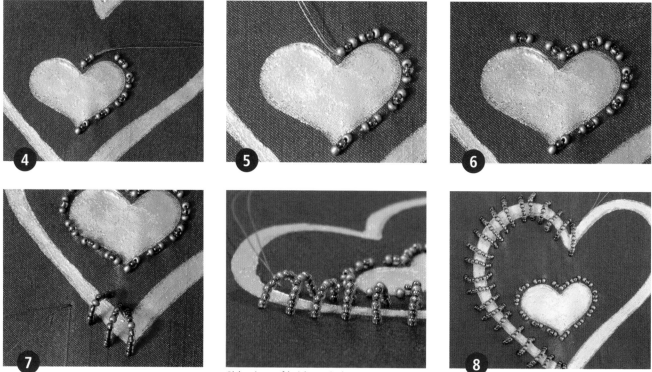

Side view of bridge stitches.

4 Work beading around small heart until you reach the top of the first lobe. Complete the stitch. Move needle (at back of fabric) to center of heart between lobes, and bring out to front. Work stitches back toward previous stitching. This will ensure you land a stitch at the center of the heart top.

5 Bring needle up and run through stitch at top center of heart emerging at center bead.

6 Add one blue and one copper bead and complete center stitch, continuing around heart in original direction. Continue adding three-bead lazy stitches to finish framing the small heart.

7 Embellish the large heart: Bring needle out inside of tip at bottom. Pick up beads in the following order: four blue, one copper and four blue. Take needle across stamped line and into fabric, letting the beads arch and stand up away from fabric, bridging the stamped image. At back of fabric, move needle over ¼" and bring up (staying on same side of painted line as you last went down). Pick up previous bead sequence, and take down next to beginning of first stitch inside the image. Move needle ¼" away at back of fabric and come up to start next stitch. Continue around outer heart image.

8 At back of fabric and at top of heart, jump over to the center to make a bridge and work backward to meet the other bridges you've stitched. This will ensure that you land a stitch at the center of the heart and maintain the spacing. When you've completed half the heart, move to the right of center top and continue down the remaining side.

Sun

1 Apply fabric paint to sun stamp and stamp image on fabric.

2 Anchor needle at back of fabric and bring out at edge of central circle. Pick up six orange beads and begin back-stitching (page 42) around edge.

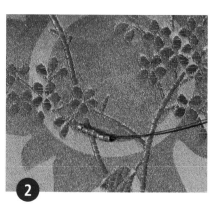

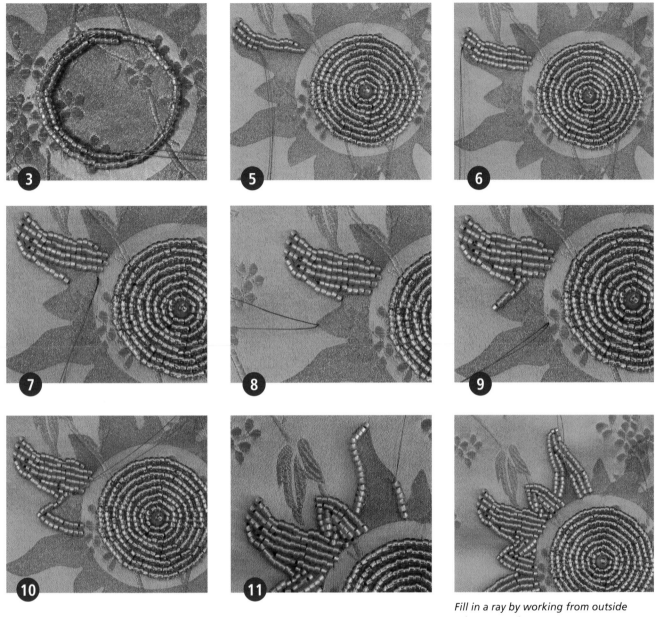

Fill in a ray by working from outside edges toward center.

3 Backstitch row by row to fill in circle. As you near the center, stop and stitch a size 5/0 orange rocaille in the center, using a size 11/0 bead to hold in place (see stacked bead stitch, page 19). Continue beading in concentric rows to surround the stack.

4 Using fuchsia beads, backstitch rays.

5 There are a couple of ways to fill in the rays. Try any of the following to determine your preferred method. The first is to backstitch rows side by side as shown.

6 As you approach the opposite side of the ray, backstitch a row to follow the outer edge of the ray rather than hugging the previous row.

7 Fill in the remainder of the ray by backstitching the gap between rows.
The alternate way to cover the rays is to outline them first, then fill in, as follows.

8 Bring needle out at tip of neighboring ray and backstitch to meet first ray.

9 Bring needle out at base of ray, opposite side.

10 Backstitch to outline the ray, then add rows to fill in, following outline.

11 Using the method you desire, fill in the rays.

BEJEWELED VASE PATCH

I'm always looking for ways to use my library of beloved clip art in fabric projects. My collection came in handy when I couldn't figure out what images would work best with hot-fix rhinestones. Going through the clip art library and looking for images with dots was the solution.

Scan the Image

1 Using your computer, scan the vase image on page 127 and place it on a document page. Test print a piece of paper first, and if satisfactory, print onto the fabric. Use the electric rhinestone applicator to affix rhinestones to the lavender dots cascading from the vase. Fuse interfacing to wrong side of fabric.

materials

- Vase image, page 127
- 8½" x 11" inkjet-printable fabric
- 5" square fusible interfacing
- 60 clear silver-backed 3 mm hot-fix rhinestones
- Size 15/0 lavender matte seed beads
- Size 15/0 seed beads: light pink, dark pink, light blue, dark blue
- Size 15 beading needle
- Beading thread
- Scissors
- Electric rhinestone applicator
- Computer with scanner and inkjet printer

techniques

Once I found clip art I liked, I used my image manipulation software to transform black-and-white line art into the colored and embossed image. I was able to size the image so the dots cascading from the flowers fit my 3 mm rhinestones. After printing out the fabric and heat setting the rhinestones, I found places to add seed beads, making the motif more dimensional.

bead quantities

Bead quantities are less than one teaspoon/5 grams/500 beads for each type, unless otherwise noted. Colors are your choice. Thread quantities are less than a skein or spool, unless otherwise noted. Please read the information in Chapter 1 before starting your project.

Tassel Flowers

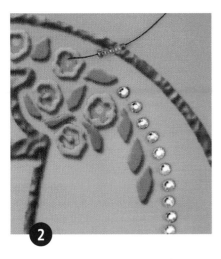

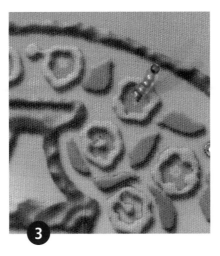

2 Anchor single strand of beading thread at back of fabric and bring out through center of a pink flower. Pick up four light pink and one dark pink size 15/0 beads.

3 Take needle back through light pink beads. Make stitch at back of fabric.

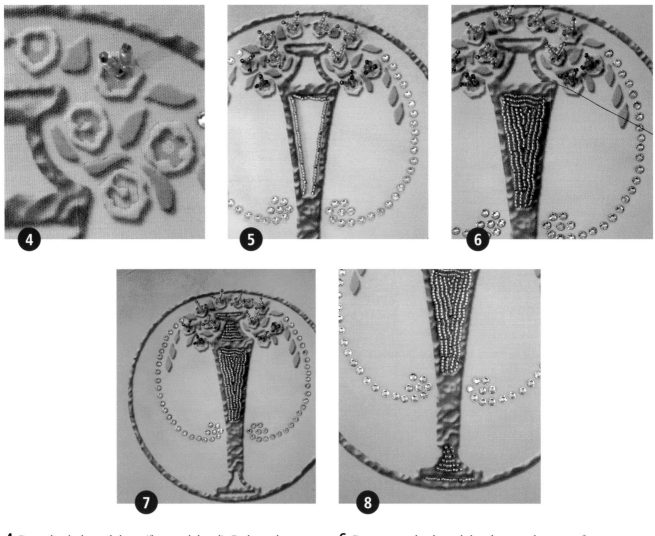

4 Come back through base (first pink bead). Pick up three light pink beads and one dark pink bead. Return through light pink beads, including base bead, to the back of fabric and take stitch. Come back up through base bead once more. Pick up four light pink beads and one dark pink bead. Return through light pink beads (including base) and make stitch at back of fabric. Stitch remaining pink blossoms, making tassel flowers in center of each pink flower, each having three beaded strands — one strand one bead longer than the other two. Stitch tassel flowers in blue blossom centers, using blue beads instead of pink.

5 Starting at outer edges, backstitch lavender matte beads around inside of main vase area.

6 Continue to backstitch beads toward center of main vase section until the area is filled in with beads.

7 Fill in top section of vase by backstitching one horizontal row of beads. Fill in section between top and main areas of vase by backstitching horizontal rows of beads to cover background.

8 Backstitch horizontal rows of beads at bottom sections of vase.

FEATHERSTITCH PATCH

This patch combines embroidered and beaded featherstitching. The free-form technique can be used as a stand-alone motif or filler in a crazy quilt. It looks great sprawled across more than one patch.

materials

- 5½" square batik fabric
- 5" square fusible interfacing
- Size 5 embroidery thread: variegated blues and pale yellows
- Size 11/0 green seed beads
- Size 11/0 pale blue seed beads
- Embroidery needle
- Beading thread
- Size 10 or 11 beading needle
- Iron and ironing board
- Scissors

techniques

Review the basic featherstitch embroidery technique (page 16). The batik fabric shown here is a real sun-printed fabric from Africa. I found it at a quilt show — a great place to find and collect all sorts of trims and fabrics for your projects. Remember, you don't need a large quantity of any one material for crazy quilting. I highly recommend attending a quilt show for both inspiration and shopping opportunities.

bead quantities

Bead quantities are less than one teaspoon/5 grams/500 beads for each type, unless otherwise noted. Colors are your choice. Thread quantities are less than a skein or spool, unless otherwise noted. Please read the information in Chapter 1 before starting your project.

Featherstitch Branches

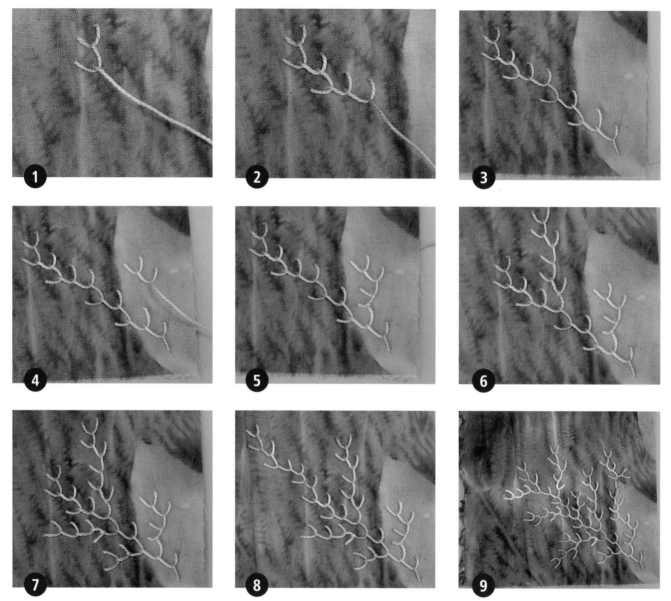

1 Fuse interfacing to wrong side of fabric. Using embroidery thread and needle, begin featherstitch (page 16) in the center of the patch. Make second featherstitch, angling the direction for the row toward the bottom right corner of the patch.

2 Continue row of stitching. It's fine to make two stitches at same side of row, as shown here, for interest and making the pattern more "organic." We will call this row the "first branch."

3 End stitching ½" from edge of fabric.

4 Begin a new row of stitching slightly above and to the right of the first row.

5 Continue stitching, aiming toward the bottom right corner, until you join up with a "twig" on the first branch of stitching.

Make a short stitch to finish this branch. Knot off thread at back of fabric.

6 Start a third branch further up in the patch and join it to the original branch.

7 Add more branches, this time starting them to the left of the first branch. The nature of a free-form design is that it evolves as you go along. Now it seems logical to make the entire motif reach further up into the patch.

8 Extend the first branch by stitching an inch or two above it, continuing in the same direction until you join the original row of stitching.

9 Continue adding branches until your stitching looks full and lush.

Beaded Featherstitch Branches

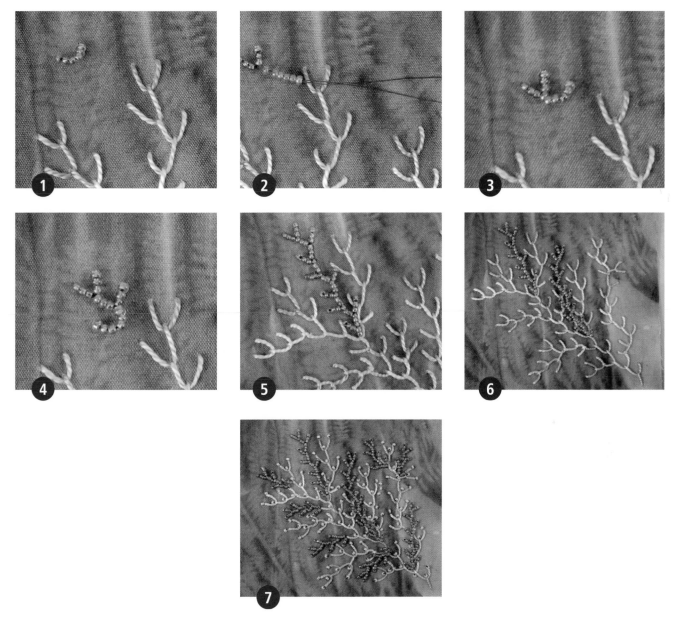

1 The next few branches are made up of featherstitched seed beads. Start the first branch by anchoring doubled beading thread at back of fabric. Bring it through the front, toward the top of the motif, in an open area between embroidered branches. Pick up six green beads and take needle down through fabric, allowing the beads to form a shallow "U."

2 Bring needle up at center of "U" and pick up six green beads.

3 Make a second stitch to right of first stitch.

4 Make third stitch to left of second stitch.

5 Continue making stitches to form a branch and connect it to the thread-embroidered branch.

6 Add another beaded branch.

7 Continue adding beaded branches to fill out the motif. Single stitch pale blue seeds at ends of thread stitches.

RIBBONS AND FIBERS PATCH

Collecting fibers, yarns, trims and ribbons of all kinds is not only fun at the time of discovery, but rewarding and useful when it comes to crazy quilting. Learn how to make a motif using narrow ribbon, narrow braid trim and fat twisted yarn, plus a few beads, of course!

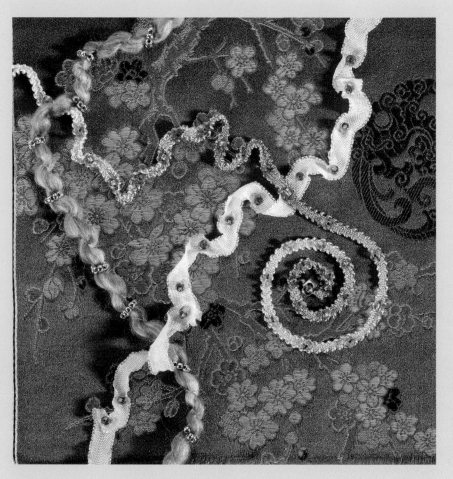

Attach Ribbons and Fibers

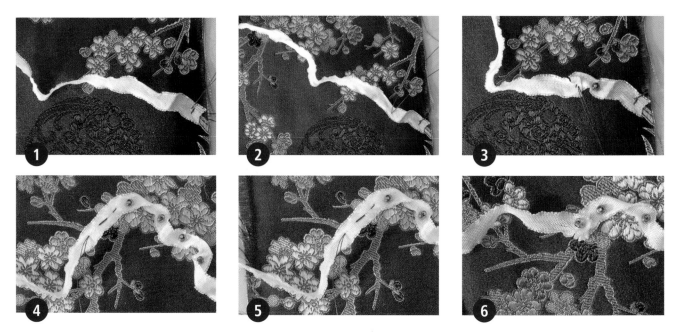

materials

- 5½" square fabric
- 4½" square fusible interfacing
- 18" pale green ¼"- to ⅜"-wide crinkly ribbon
- 24" multicolored narrow ³⁄₁₆" braid
- 8" fat twisted blue yarn
- Metallic green cube bead
- Green size 5/0 or 6/0 rocailles
- Green size 11/0 seed beads
- Metallic gold size 11/0 seed beads
- Size 10 or 11 beading needle
- Beading thread
- Scissors
- Iron and ironing board

techniques

When using this technique in a multi-patch project, take one or more of the trims across neighboring quilt patches (as shown on the canister wrapper on page 53). Every trim you stitch down becomes a surface to which beads can (and should!) be added.

bead quantities

Bead quantities are less than one teaspoon/5 grams/500 beads for each type, unless otherwise noted. Colors are your choice. Thread quantities are less than a skein or spool, unless otherwise noted. Please read the information in Chapter 1 before starting your project.

1 Fuse interfacing to fabric. Using doubled beading thread, tack end of crinkly ribbon to edge of patch at seam allowance.

2 At back of fabric, move needle over ½" and come up through fabric and ribbon.
Note: the ribbon need not lie flat against the fabric; it is more interesting if it buckles up a bit.

3 Pick up rocaille and gold metallic bead and stitch bead stack (page 19) through ribbon and fabric. Scrunch ribbon toward last stitch and hold in place with thumbnail. At back of fabric, move needle over a fraction of an inch and bring back up through layers of scrunched ribbon. Take a small stitch through ribbon and fabric to secure.

4 Add a new bead stack on top of stitch from previous step. Continue scrunching, folding and twisting the ribbon to add dimension and texture, stitching bead stacks every so often to hold ribbon in place. Let the ribbon meander across the patch, following a random path.

5 Bring needle up through ribbon and take a few running stitches in ribbon only.

6 Pull ribbon up to gather. Stitch to fabric with bead stack.

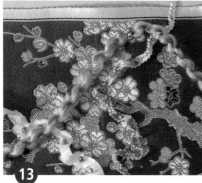

7 Continue beading and stitching ribbon to opposite edge of patch.
Note: Keep beads out of seam allowance, but tack ends of fibers with thread inside seam allowances near edge of fabric. Knot off thread at back in seam allowance. Trim excess ribbon at edge of patch.

8 Tack end of narrow braid trim to fabric.

9 Bring needle up through stitch and pick up cube and size 11/0 green bead. Stitch bead stack through braid and secure at back of fabric. Fold braid next to stack and bring needle up through both layers of braid. Stitch to fabric using a size 11/0 green seed bead.

10 Coil braid around stack and stitch to fabric at short intervals with seed beads. Fold braid and make tight curves as necessary. After several turns, let the tail of the spiral spill across the crinkly ribbon and stitch through all the layers of braid, ribbon and fabric.

11 Stitch braid trim to its own meandering path across the patch, twisting, buckling and bending it as you go. Remember — avoid beading into seam allowance. Knot off and trim braid at edge of patch.

12 Lay length of yarn across patch and shape as desired. Let it cross over the ribbon and braid trim paths.

13 Couch (page 24) yarn to fabric using metallic gold beads. Trim ends of yarn along patch edges.

BEADED LAVENDER SPRIGS PATCH

I learned to make lavender sprays using a silk ribbon embroidery method that was difficult, tedious and consumed lots of ribbon. Not wanting to give up on a lavender motif, I came up with my own rendition using beads. Embroider the stems and learn a beading stitch to create the buds. You could create the same stitches with different colored threads and beads to make a completely different bouquet.

materials

- Sprigs pattern, page 122
- 5½" square fabric
- 5" square fusible interfacing
- 13" length of multicolored ¼"- to ⅜"- wide ribbon
- Size 5 green perle cotton embroidery thread
- 2 to 3 strands bright purple size 11/0 seed beads
- Embroidery needle
- Size 11 (or smaller) beading needle
- Beading thread
- Fine-tip black permanent fabric marker
- Iron and ironing board
- Air-erasable fabric marker
- Light table or other light source
- Scissors
- Ruler or tape measure

techniques

The beaded lazy daisy is just like the embroidered version (page 22) but with beaded thread. You can make more delicate flower buds by using size 15/0 beads. This quilt patch also offers a way to use a pretty hand-dyed ribbon and lovely batik fabric together. The ribbon softens the motif and adds more color. Once you learn how easy and gratifying it is to make this motif, you'll be all set to try your own variations.

bead quantities

Bead quantities are less than one teaspoon/5 grams/500 beads for each type, unless otherwise noted. Colors are your choice. Thread quantities are less than a skein or spool, unless otherwise noted. Please read the information in Chapter 1 before starting your project.

Trace Pattern

1 Trace pattern onto non-adhesive side of fusible interfacing with permanent marker. Fuse interfacing to wrong side of fabric.

2 Place patch on light table or other source of light and retrace pattern on right side of fabric using air-erasable marker. Stitch the stems using either split stitch (page 73) or stem stitch (page 22) or a combination of both.

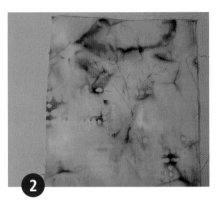

Embroider the Stems

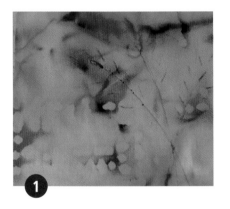

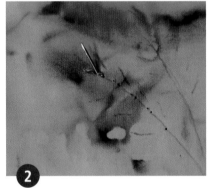

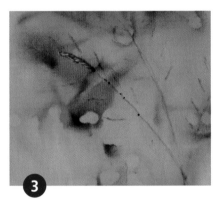

1 Using embroidery needle and perle cotton knotted at back of fabric, make first split stitch at one end of a stem.

2 Pierce through thread of first stitch to begin second split stitch.

3 Make second split stitch, working toward bottom end of stem.

4 Finish first stem. At back of fabric, bring needle up at bottom of second stem and work split or stem stitches up to top of stem.

5 Stitch third stem, knot off at back of fabric and trim tail of thread.

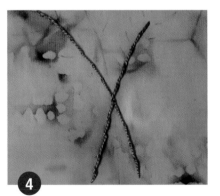

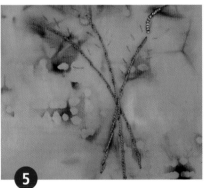

Bead the Buds

Note: Pattern lines for buds indicate direction of stitches as a general guide; you should not try to place a bud at each drawn line from pattern.

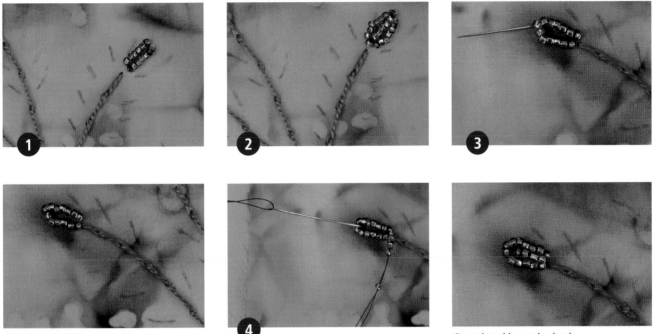

Completed odd-number bead loop.

Completed lavender bud.

1 Near the top end of a stem, anchor doubled beading thread at back of fabric. Bring to front of fabric and pick up 12 beads.

2 Make a beaded lazy daisy stitch (see diagram): Insert needle into fabric, next to the first bead, and pull thread to form a loop of beads. Bring needle up inside end of loop, go across threads in loop, and take needle down into fabric to secure end of beaded loop to the patch.

3 Bring needle up inside base of loop, pick up five beads, and take needle down inside top of loop to form bud.

4 The second option for making buds uses an odd number (in this case, 11) beads to form the loop. Bring needle up through middle (sixth bead) at end of loop and go back down into fabric to secure loop to patch.

BEAD STITCH
Lazy Daisy

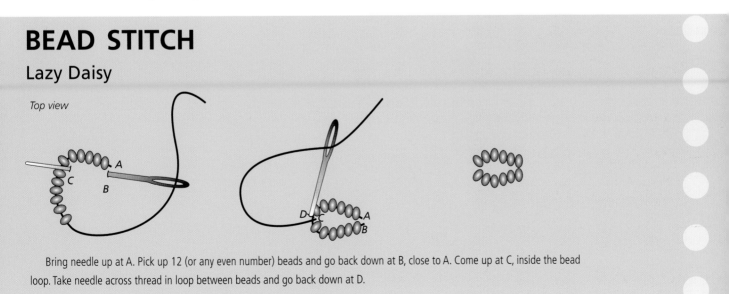

Top view

Bring needle up at A. Pick up 12 (or any even number) beads and go back down at B, close to A. Come up at C, inside the bead loop. Take needle across thread in loop between beads and go back down at D.

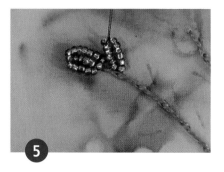

5

6

All three stems filled with buds.

5 Fill in center of odd loop as in Step 4, using four beads.

6 Work down the stem, adding buds using even or odd bead loops.

7 Alternate from side to side, filling each stem with buds.

Tie it up with a Pretty Bow

1

2

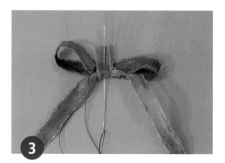

3

4

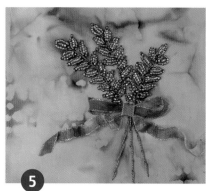

5

1 Cut a 1" ribbon piece and set aside. Fold remaining 12" ribbon in half. Using beading thread, stitch ribbon together 2½" from fold.

2 Form end of ribbon into two loops and stitch on top of previous stitch to hold in place.

3 Wrap 1" piece of ribbon (set aside earlier) around center of bow and stitch at back to hold in place. Knot off and trim thread tails.

4 Place bow onto patch at intersection of the three stems. With beading thread anchored at back of fabric, stitch bow to center of patch.

5 Shape bow loops and tails. Use tiny stitches to tack to the patch in a pleasing arrangement. Trim ribbon ends along patch edges.

SILK RIBBON FLOWERS PATCH

A dragonfly floating above a summer garden abloom with color — this lively and colorful quilt patch would be lovely on any crazy quilt or small accessory. Learn a few easy silk ribbon embroidery stitches to make the flowers and leaves on embroidered perle cotton stems. Construct a dimensional dragonfly with beaded body to round out the motif.

materials

- Patterns, page 125
- 5½" square green fabric
- 5" square fusible interfacing
- Size 8 perle cotton: one or two shades of green
- 4 mm silk embroidery ribbon: lavender, purple, pale yellow, green, magenta, blue
- 7 mm silk embroidery ribbon: variegated pink, dark green
- Pink size 11/0 seed beads
- Purple size 11/0 seed beads
- Orange size 8/0 seed beads
- 16" green 26-gauge wire
- 2 teal 2" squares organza fabric or ribbon
- 3 mm or 3.5 mm green iridescent beads
- ⅜" purple cylinder bead
- 2 small green bugle beads
- Embroidery needle
- Size 10 or smaller beading needle
- Beading thread
- Iron-on adhesive
- Silver metallic sewing thread
- Fine-tip black permanent fabric marker
- Iron and ironing board
- Parchment to protect ironing board
- Tracing paper
- Air-erasable fabric marker
- Scissors
- Wire cutter or nail clippers
- Round nose pliers or skewer

techniques

When selecting the background fabric for this patch, choose solids or very subtle prints to show off the colorful ribbon embroidery. If you like, interchange your favorite ribbon colors to make your own unique garden. With these few simple stitches, you can design a different garden for every crazy quilt project you make.

bead quantities

Bead quantities are less than one teaspoon/5 grams/500 beads for each type, unless otherwise noted. Colors are your choice. Thread quantities are less than a skein or spool, unless otherwise noted. Please read the information in Chapter 1 before starting your project.

Pattern

1 Trace garden pattern onto non-adhesive side of interfacing using permanent marker. Fuse interfacing to wrong side of fabric. Use the pattern as a general placement guide for stitching the garden.

Stitch Silk Ribbon Flowers

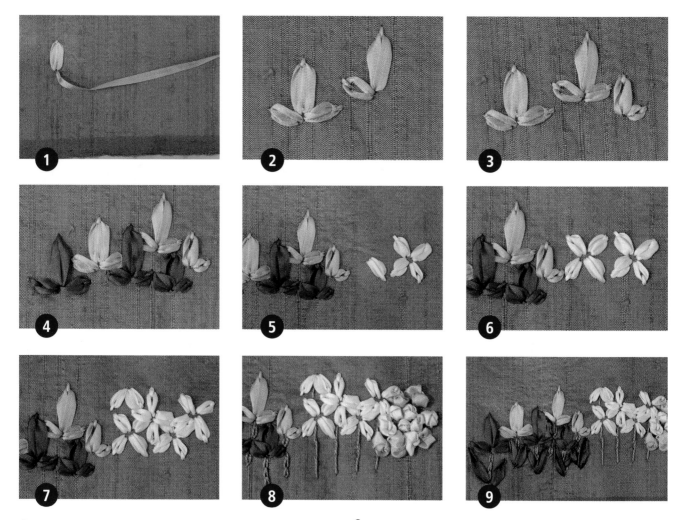

1 Using lavender ribbon in embroidery needle, make a vertical lazy daisy stitch (page 105) to start first iris flower.

2 Make smaller lazy daisy stitches at each side of first stitch. Start second iris at right of first one.

3 Start third iris at right of second one, making only the two stitches shown.

4 Switch to purple ribbon and stitch three more iris blossoms.

5 Use pale yellow ribbon to make first four-petaled flower using lazy daisy stitch. Start second yellow flower between first one and iris.

6 Finish second yellow flower.

7 Add two and a half additional yellow flowers above the first two.

8 Using pink variegated ribbon, stitch 10 or 11 loose French knots (page 105) to right of yellow flowers. Using perle cotton, embroider split stitch stems (page 73) below yellow flowers and small chain stitch (page 105) stems below iris blossoms.

9 Using dark green 7 mm silk ribbon, add ribbon stitch leaves (page 73) to iris.

SILK RIBBON EMBROIDERY

Lazy Daisy

Bring needle up at A. Go back down at B right next to A to form a small loop. Come back up at C, inside of ribbon loop. Take needle back down at D to hold end of loop in place against fabric.

French Knot

Bring needle up at A. Wrap ribbon around needle one or more times, pull snug and go back down at B, right next to A.

Note: If ribbon is wrapped in wrong direction, the stitch will disappear.

EMBROIDERY STITCH

Chain Stitch

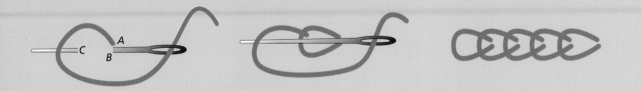

Bring needle up at A. Go back down at B, right next to A, to form a loop. Come back up at C, inside of loop. Take needle back down next to C, inside of loop, and come back up through second loop; repeat.

Completed magenta flowers.

10 Use 4 mm green silk ribbon to add ribbon stitch leaves to yellow flowers and tiny lazy daisy leaves to pink flowers.

11 Single stitch an orange size 8/0 bead to center of each yellow flower.

12 Single stitch a purple bead at center of each iris. Add three split-stitch stems behind yellow flowers using green perle cotton.

13 Starting at top of new stem and using blue silk ribbon, plume stitch (see diagram) down one side of stem.

14 Begin each plume stitch by bringing needle out through bottom of previous stitch.

15 Plume stitch down opposite side of stem, then start at top and plume stitch down the center.

16 Plume stitch the remaining two stems. Featherstitch (page 16) three new stems behind the iris using perle cotton. With magenta silk ribbon, stitch a combination of tiny lazy daisy stitches and tight French knots at end of each featherstitch to resemble blossoms and unopened buds.

17 Continue working the magenta ribbon flowers toward left of patch, filling in behind iris.

SILK RIBBON EMBROIDERY
Plume Stitch

Stitch from right to left or top to bottom. Bring needle up at A and go back down at B. Leave a loop of ribbon on top of fabric and insert a skewer or similar object to hold it in place. Bring needle up at C, piercing the end of the first ribbon stitch. Take needle down at D to start next stitch.

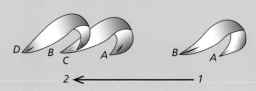

Dragonfly

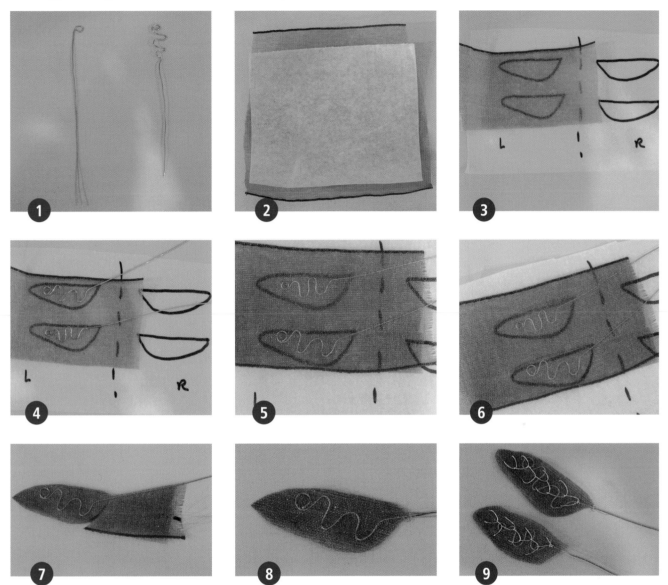

1 Cut wire into four 4" pieces. Use round nose pliers or skewer to bend a small circle at one end of each wire. Bend each wire back and forth a few times to make a wavy pattern in the same end as the circle.

2 Protect your ironing board with parchment in case some of the adhesive seeps through the organza. Fuse iron-on adhesive to one side of organza squares. Remove paper liner.

3 Trace wings pattern onto tracing paper. Place tracing on protected ironing board. Cut one organza square in half. Place one piece on top of wing pattern, adhesive side up.

4 Position a shaped wire on each wing so its straight tail extends from point of wing as shown. The wire shape must fit within the wing outline, so adjust and reshape it accordingly.

5 Place remaining piece of organza over wings, adhesive side down. Press to fuse organza layers together, sandwiching the shaped wires in between. Let cool.

6 Trace wing shape onto organza using air-erasable marker.

7 Carefully cut out wing shapes leaving the area around wire tail for last.

8 Cut fabric as close to wire tail as possible and remove as much of the organza as you can without disturbing the wing. Repeat Steps 2 through 8 to create the second pair of wings.

9 Using metallic sewing thread and beading needle, feather stitch through all layers of wings, capturing the wire shapes as shown.

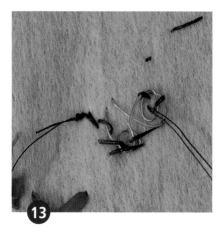

10 Create the dragonfly body: Stitch round, cylinder and bugle beads to patch, referring to pattern on back for position.

11 Poke ends of one pair of wing wires into fabric near the dragonfly head. If the wire ends don't easily penetrate the fabric, use an embroidery needle to make a pilot hole.

12 Insert wings into fabric until organza is against the surface of the patch. At back of patch, bend the wire ends into tight loops and flatten them against the fabric.

13 Secure wings by stitching wire end loops to interfacing layer only.

14 Repeat Steps 11 through 13 to attach second pair of wings.

SAMPLER SQUARE

Combine motif blocks you've created with novelty fabrics to make a small sampler that could be a wall hanging or cover for an end table. Make it as simple or elaborate as you like. This piece is a manageable size for a first project and it will give you an idea of how large or small you'll want to make your future projects.

materials

- 13½" square fusible fleece or other foundation
- Assorted patches of novelty fabrics
- Stitched motif patches
- Assorted colors size 8 Fine Braid metallic thread
- Size 5 assorted colors embroidery thread
- Size 8 assorted colors perle cotton embroidery thread
- Assorted colors size 11/0 seed beads
- Assorted colors size 15/0 seed beads
- Assorted colors size 5/0 or 6/0 rocaille beads
- Assorted colors and sizes of bugle beads
- Assorted colors of small decorative beads, such as teardrops and daggers
- Leaf-shaped beads
- Spider silver charm
- 3 mm bead (dragonfly head)
- Oval focal bead (dragonfly body)
- 4 dagger beads (dragonfly wings)
- Assorted ribbons, fibers and trims
- 2 yd. of 2½"-wide fabric strips or ribbon
- 15½" square backing fabric
- Permanent fabric marker
- Beading needle
- Beading thread
- Ruler
- Iron and ironing board
- Embroidery needle
- Dress or straight pins
- Scissors
- Sewing thread and needle
- Optional: sewing machine

techniques

High-tech meets low-tech! This sampler is made using basic needle and thread technology that's been around for thousands of years. My 21st century digital camera allowed me to take progressive shots of each step as I went along. I confess, the low-tech time I spent was far more satisfying! And there's no certain order to follow once you start the stitching, this just happens to be the order in which I did things, completely random and unplanned. Remember to turn and hold your project for the best vantage point when stitching (which is why a few of the photos seem to be upside down). I always start at the outer edges and work inward, removing pins as I go to easily access the interior without fighting the pins. For the same reason, I prefer to embroider all of my seams first, then go back and add trims and beads after the pins are out of the way.

bead quantities

Bead quantities are less than one teaspoon/5 grams/500 beads for each type, unless otherwise noted. Colors are your choice. Thread quantities are less than a skein or spool, unless otherwise noted. Please read the information in Chapter 1 before starting your project.

Arrange the Quilt Patches

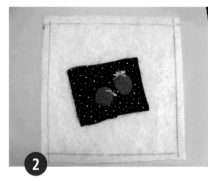

Fleece foundation entirely covered with patches.

1 Draw ½" seam allowance around non-adhesive side of fusible fleece square using fabric marker. Refer to this line often so you don't extend your stitching into the seam allowance.

2 Select motif patch for sampler center and determine approximate location on fleece.

3 Place additional motifs or fabric patches around center patch. Place pins in the patches you want to remain in place.

4 Turn under edges of topmost patches where they overlap by at least ½" and pin in place.

5 Continue to arrange patches, turning edges under on the ones that overlap others, and pin as you go

Embroider the Seams

The stitching along the seams is decorative, but also attaches the seams to each other and to the foundation. By using this (my preferred) method for seaming, you won't have to baste or sew the seams first; you can start right in with the fun part!

The first seam is stitched and a pin has been removed.

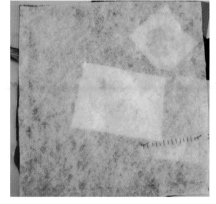

The stitches go through all layers, including the foundation, as shown here from the back.

1 The blanket stitch (page 16) is an easy stitch to start with. Make the first two stitches on the patch in the lower left corner of my sampler along the fold where it overlaps the patch above it. Stitch through all the layers, including the foundation.

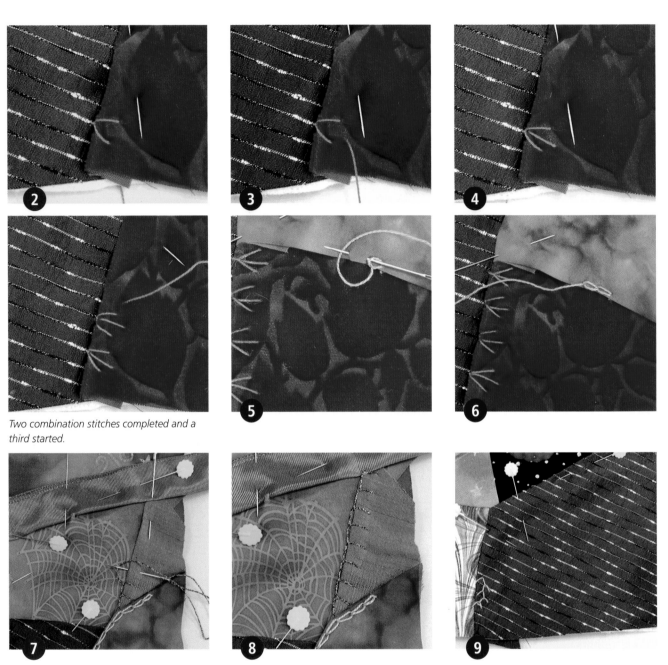

Two combination stitches completed and a third started.

Blanket stitched seam completed.

2 Randomly, I selected the lower right corner patch as my next seam to stitch, and decided to make a simple combination stitch. Start with a fly stitch (page 16) and make individual fly stitches side by side along the seam rather than a vertical line of stitching. Each fly stitch has a very short tail, which makes the stitch look like a "V."

3 The second part of this combination stitch is a straight stitch (page 113). Bring needle up through the fabric above and between the legs of the fly stitch.

4 The straight stitch ends in the valley of the fly stitch, completing the first combination stitch.

5 Start chain stitch at edge of third seam.

6 Stitch to the corner and continue stitching up the side and across the top of this patch using a chain stitch.

7 Blanket stitch the adjacent patch with metallic Fine Braid.

8 This small patch is close to the outer edge of the sampler. An extra pin placed in the seam allowance will remind you to keep the stitching far enough away from the edge.

9 Move over to another seam at the bottom of the sampler and make a featherstitched border.

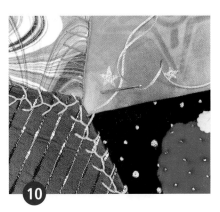

Featherstitch seam completed.

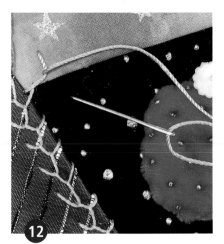

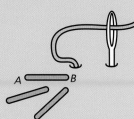

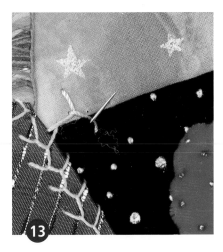

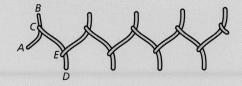

10 Stitch the next seam using a cretan stitch (see diagram). Start at the edge and bring needle out, then take back into fabric as shown.

11 Bring needle up between beginning and ending of first part of stitch, similar to making a fly stitch.

12 Move needle into adjoining patch about ¼" from seam and take down through fabric.

13 Bring needle back up midway along last stitch.

EMBROIDERY STITCHES

Straight Stitch

Bring needle up at A, take back down at B. Make the length and angle whatever you like.

Cretan Stitch

Bring needle up at A, take back down at B and bring back up at C, keeping thread under the point of the needle. Go back down at D, come back up at E. Work from left to right.

EMBROIDERY STITCHES

Sheaf Stitch

Make three evenly spaced parallel straight stitches. Bring needle up at center and take thread around the stitches, cinching the straight stitches in the middle, and take needle back down at center.

Herringbone Stitch

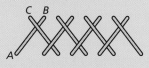

Bring needle up at A, take back down at B. Bring back up at C, left of B, to start next stitch.

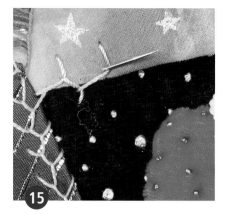

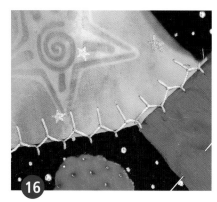

Cretan stitch seam completed.

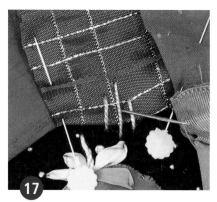

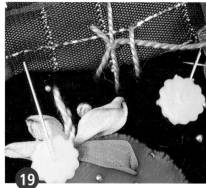

14 Move needle back to first patch about ¼" from seam and take needle down.

15 Bring needle back up midway along last stitch.

16 Take needle down in second patch and bring back up midway along last stitch. Continue along seam.

17 To join narrow end of plaid patch to the adjacent patch, start a sheaf stitch (see diagram). Make three straight stitches parallel to each other at edge of seam, catching fabric from both patches. The center stitch is purposely made longer. Bring needle up along right side of center stitch at midpoint, as shown.

18 Take thread across center and left stitch. Slide needle (eye-end first to avoid snagging threads or fabric) behind all three stitches going from left to right.

19 Pull needle all the way through, which tightens thread across center and left stitch.

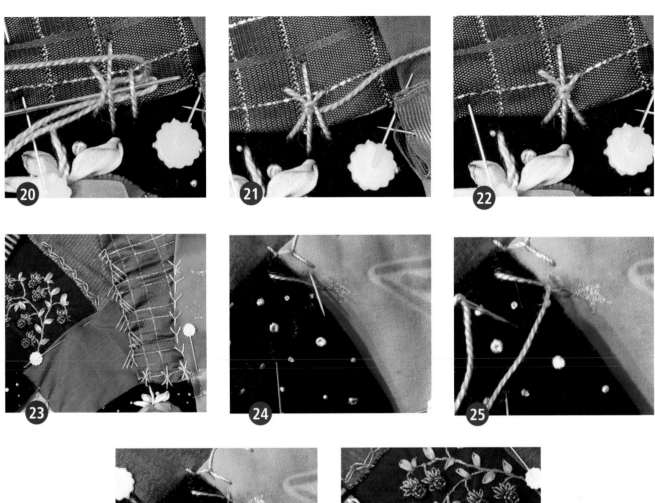

Lazy daisy trios stitched along seam.

20 Once again, take thread across all three vertical stitches. Slide needle, eye-end first, behind all three stitches going from left to right.

21 Pull needle all the way through, which tightens thread and pulls all three legs of the sheaf stitch together at center.

22 Take needle down at left side of stitch, next to center. Add more sheaf stitches to finish seam.

23 Embroider the other two seams on the plaid patch using a maidenhair stitch (page 22) along one side and fly stitch (page 16) along the other. To avoid stitching into the seam allowance at edge of fleece, keep an eye on the line you marked in Step 1.

24 Using the herringbone stitch (page 114) join the next two patches. Bring needle up near edge on one side of seam in one of the patches. Angle stitch to right and go down into the other patch. Behind the fabric, move needle back (left) a small distance and come back up on same side of seam.

25 Take another angled stitch across the seam into the first patch.

26 Move needle to left at back of sampler and come back up on same side of seam.

27 Stitch trios of lazy daisy stitches along a seam, starting each of the three stitches in the same spot.

28 Start side by side fly stitches with very short stems along the seam of a narrow patch which is actually a wide ribbon. Note that I folded this ribbon patch the long way to fit my patchwork. The other edge is left as is, since it's already a finished edge.

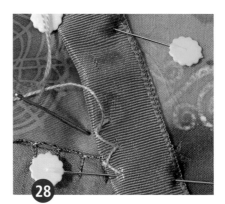

29 Bring needle out of same hole as previous stitch to connect the fly stitching and create a stitched zigzag look.

30 Stitch a wavy row of chain stitches along one side of the raspberry patch. Opposite that seam, work a variation of the blanket stitch. Make five stitches, each a bit longer than the previous one. With the fifth stitch, make each stitch shorter than the previous one.

31 After finishing the blanket stitched seam, stitch the final seam using the herringbone stitch.

Add Surface Decoration.

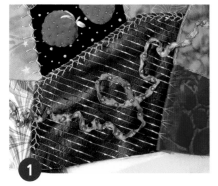

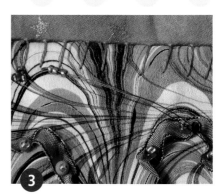

1 When all the seams are stitched down and the pins removed, fill in some of the more open areas with trims and ribbons. Using the narrow, crinkly hand-dyed ribbon, arrange a bumpy, twisted meandering path across the bottom of the sampler. Start at one side and travel across three patches, ending at the opposite edge. (I pinned it in a few key places, but for the most part just arranged and stitched as I worked.) Attach the ribbon using short bead stacks (page 19) consisting of a rocaille topped with a seed bead at approximately ½" intervals along the ribbon.

2 Tack a length of flower-ribbon trim across three other patches. As the beads are already part of the trim, hide small stitches with matching sewing thread through the flowers. Make the ribbon stand up slightly off the fabric by adjusting the tension between flowers.

3 Remember the very first seam you blanket stitched? Now go back and add seed beads. Take the beading needle and thread up at the end of each stitch and pick up three beads.

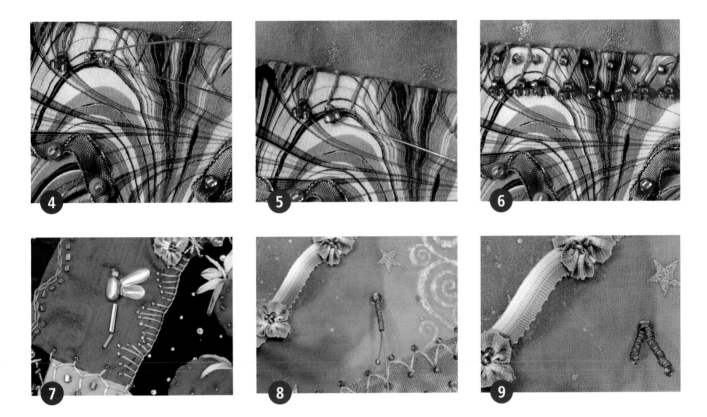

4 Take the needle back down through the first bead.

5 Bring needle back up, inside bead cluster, and stitch across thread between second and third beads.

6 Place three beads at end of each blanket stitch. Work back across the row and single stitch a bead between each blanket stitch.

7 Stitch on beads to make a dragonfly. Start with round bead

for head, followed by oval bead for body and bugles for tail. Add two daggers to sides of body for wings.

8 Beaded tassel flowers use a rocaille for the base and magenta seeds fringe with an orange seed at the end to serve as stop bead.

9 Add second strand of beads to tassel flower. See page 119 for additional beading techniques before assembly.

Assemble

1 Pin 2½"-wide strips of fabric or ribbon around the patchwork. Fold ends out of the way. Using ½" seam allowance, stitch strip to each side of the sampler, stopping and ending each seam ½" from edges of sampler.

2 Press border strips away from sampler to make a frame.

3 Press top and bottom frame ends under at 45-degree angle. Pin to frame strips beneath.

4 Finish corners: Stitch short bead stacks along seam, ending stitching ½" from edge. Trim frame ends square.

5 With right sides together, stitch sampler to back using ½" seam allowance and leaving a 4" opening at one side to turn. Trim corners.

6 Turn right-side out. Whipstitch opening closed. Press frames flat, then carefully iron over back to fuse to fleece.

7 Blanket stitch around frame going through all layers.

8 Single stitch seed beads to ends of each blanket stitch.

9 Stitch picot bead edging (see diagram and sequence) around all four sides to finish.

BEAD STITCH
Picot Edging

With beading needle and thread, anchor stitch at edge of fabric. Pick up three seed beads and follow this sequence: one orange, one purple and one orange. Take stitch next to first stitch, allowing orange beads to touch and forcing the purple bead to stand out from edge a bit. Bring needle back out through last bead stitched and pick up one purple and one orange bead. Continue around edge of sampler, finishing with a purple bead sewn between last and first orange beads stitched.

Additional Bead Decorations

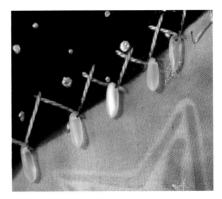

Dagger beads added to herringbone stitches.

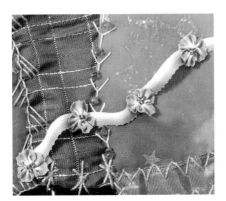

Small teardrop beads added to fly stitches.

Seed beads added to fly stitches and spider charm added to spider web patch.

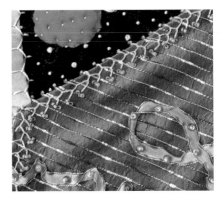

Clusters of three seed beads added to featherstitches.

Variety of bead treatments added to stitching around raspberry motif patch.

Bugle beads added to cretan and herringbone stitches.

Seed beads added to blanket and herringbone stitches around strawberry motif patch and bead stacks added between sheaf stitches.

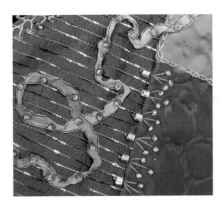

Seed beads added to chain stitching and to fly/straight stitch combination seam.

Resources

Beads and Beading Supplies

Beyond Beadery
www.beyondbeadery.com

The Bead Shop
www.mailorder-beads.co.uk

Fire Mountain Gems and Beads
www.firemountaingems.com

Micro Tube/Micro Bugle Beads
www.empyreanbeads.com
www.landofodds.com

Hot-Fix Rhinestones & Setter

Creative Crystal
www.creative-crystal.com

Metallic Embroidery Thread

Kreinik Mfg. Co.
www.kreinik.com

Trims

Flights of Fancy
www.flightsoffancyboutique.com

Fiber and Ribbon Embellishments

Embellishments!
www.fibergoddess.com

Silk Embroidery Ribbon

Bucilla
www.plaidonline.com

Hand-Dyed Embroidery Thread

The Caron Collection
www.caron-net.com

Books

KP Books
700 E. State St.
Iola, WI 54990-0001
Phone: (800) 258-0929
E-mail: BooksCustomerService@fwpubs.com

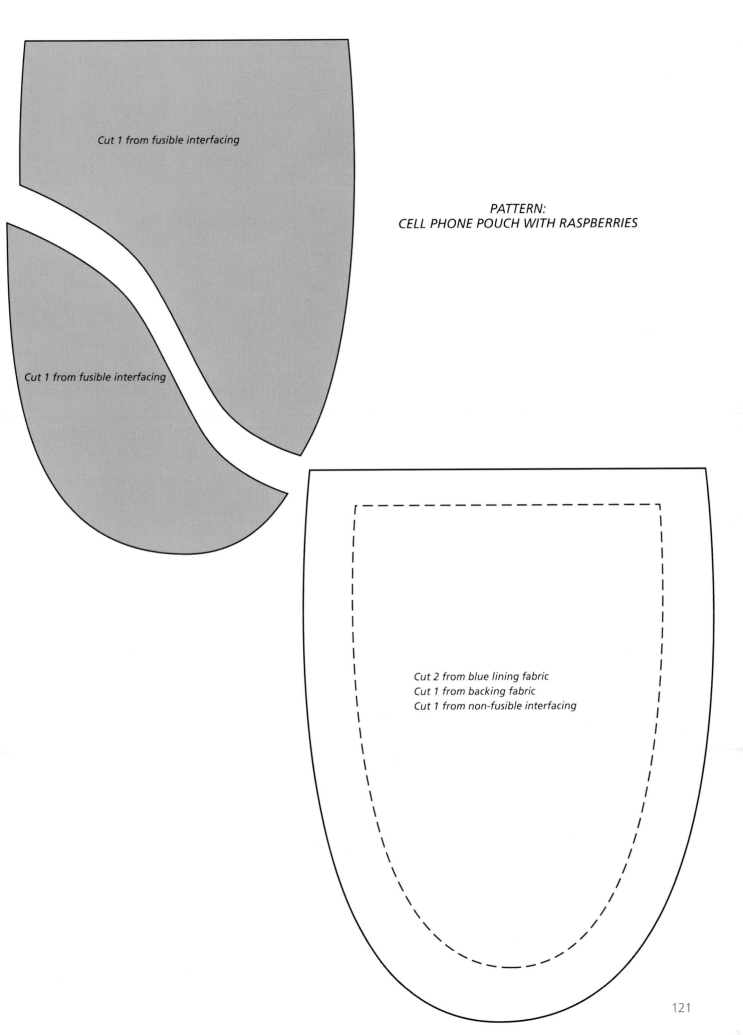

Cut 1 from fusible interfacing

Cut 1 from fusible interfacing

PATTERN:
CELL PHONE POUCH WITH RASPBERRIES

Cut 2 from blue lining fabric
Cut 1 from backing fabric
Cut 1 from non-fusible interfacing

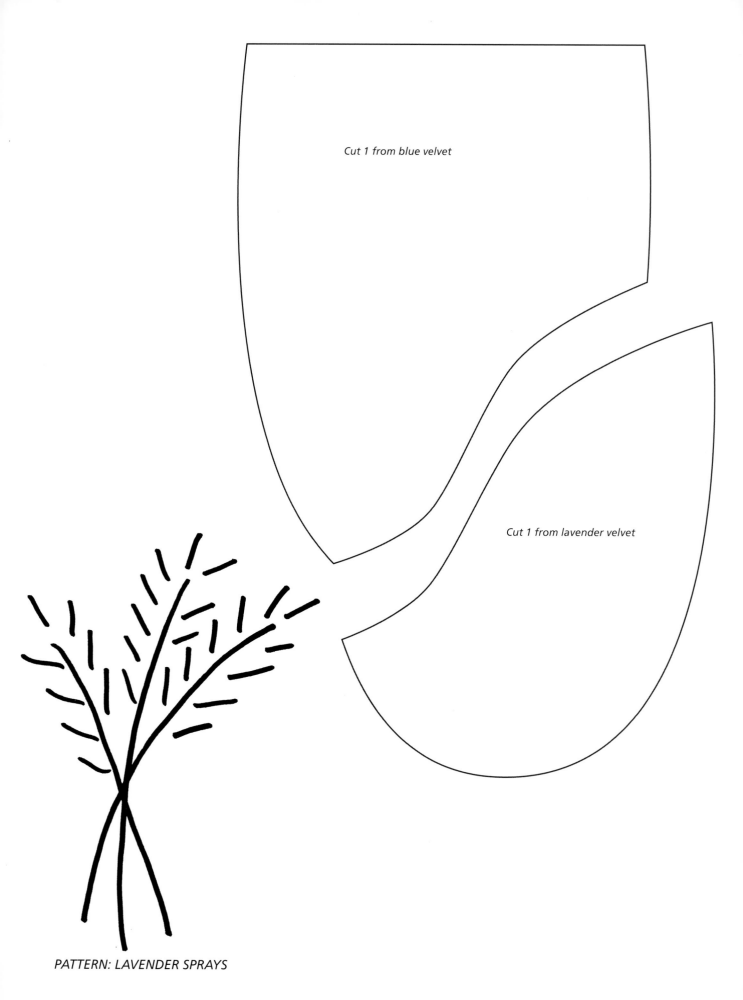

Cut 1 from blue velvet

Cut 1 from lavender velvet

PATTERN: LAVENDER SPRAYS

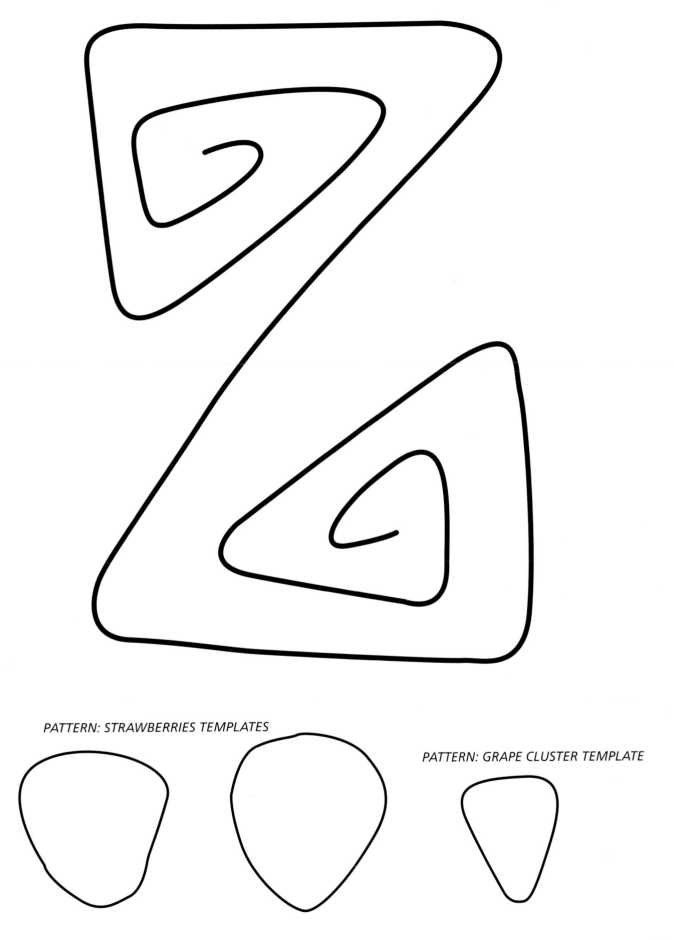

PATTERN: STRAWBERRIES TEMPLATES

PATTERN: GRAPE CLUSTER TEMPLATE

PATTERN: NAUTILUS BEADWORK
SCROLLWORK DESIGN

PATTERN: PEACOCK EYE

eye

PATTERN: GIFT BAG
SILK RIBBON SPIRAL

barb

spine

PATTERN: PEACOCK FEATHER

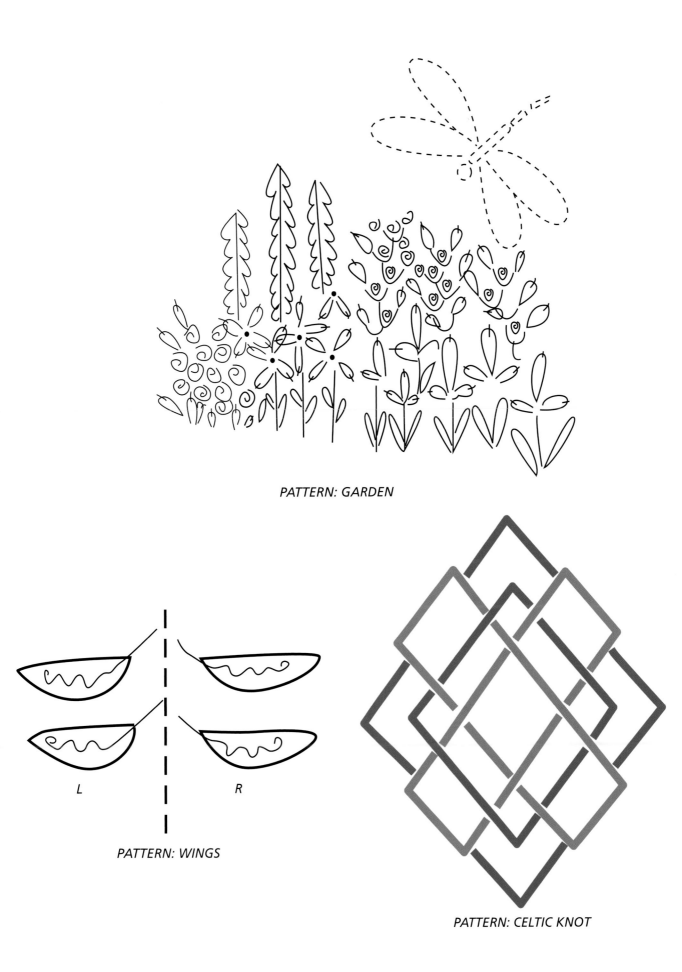

PATTERN: GARDEN

PATTERN: WINGS

L   R

PATTERN: CELTIC KNOT

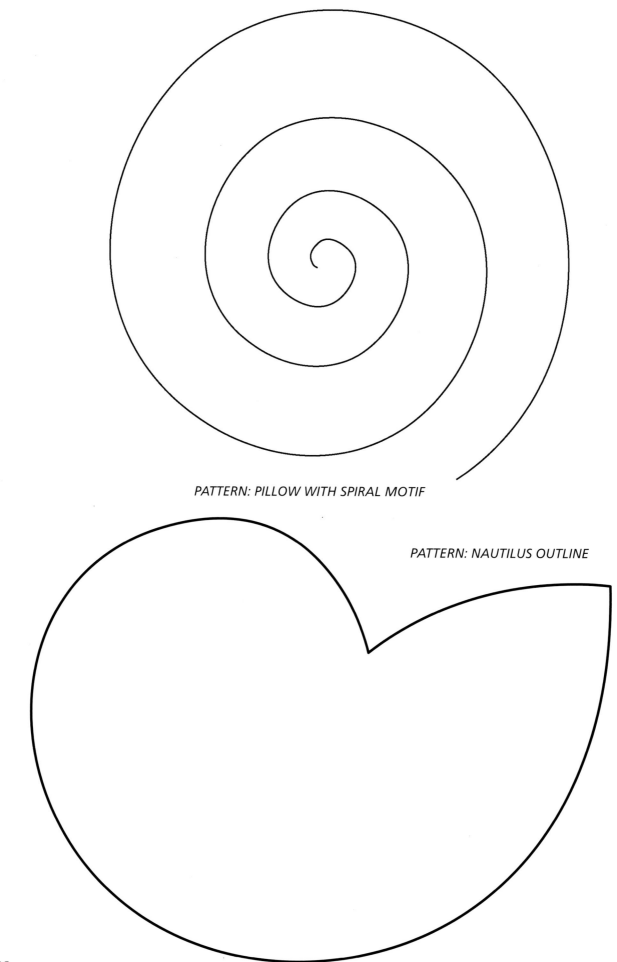

PATTERN: PILLOW WITH SPIRAL MOTIF

PATTERN: NAUTILUS OUTLINE

VASE IMAGE

WREATH IMAGE

NAUTILUS IMAGE